Sensing the Divine

The Bible Reading Fellowship
15 The Chambers, Vineyard
Abingdon OX14 3FE
brf.org.uk

The Bible Reading Fellowship (BRF) is a Registered Charity (233280)

ISBN 978 0 85746 658 7
First published 2019
10 9 8 7 6 5 4 3 2 1 0
All rights reserved

Acknowledgements
Unless otherwise acknowledged, scripture quotations are from The New Revised Standard Version of the Bible, Anglicised edition, copyright © 1989, 1995 by the Division of Christian Education of the National Council of the Churches of Christ in the United States of America. Used by permission. All rights reserved.

Scripture taken from the New Century Version®. Copyright © 2005 by Thomas Nelson. Used by permission. All rights reserved. • Scripture quotations are taken from The Message, copyright © 1993, 1994, 1995, 1996, 2000, 2001, 2002 by Eugene H. Peterson. Used by permission of NavPress. All rights reserved. Represented by Tyndale House Publishers, Inc. • Extracts from the Authorised Version of the Bible (The King James Bible), the rights in which are vested in the Crown, are reproduced by permission of the Crown's Patentee, Cambridge University Press. • Scripture quotations taken from The Holy Bible, New International Version (Anglicised edition) copyright © 1979, 1984, 2011 by Biblica. Used by permission of Hodder & Stoughton Publishers, an Hachette UK company. All rights reserved. 'NIV' is a registered trademark of Biblica. UK trademark number 1448790. • Scripture quotations from the Contemporary English Version. New Testament © American Bible Society 1991, 1992, 1995. Old Testament © American Bible Society 1995. Anglicisations © British & Foreign Bible Society 1996. Used by permission. • The Living Bible copyright © 1971 by Tyndale House Foundation. Used by permission of Tyndale House Publishers Inc., Carol Stream, Illinois 60188. All rights reserved. • Scripture quotations taken from the Amplified® Bible (AMPC), Copyright © 1954, 1958, 1962, 1964, 1965, 1987 by The Lockman Foundation. Used by permission. www.Lockman.org. • Scripture quotations from the Good News Bible (GNT) published by The Bible Societies/HarperCollins Publishers Ltd, UK © American Bible Society 1966, 1971, 1976, 1992, used with permission. • Quotations from the Jubilee Bible Copyright © 2000, 2001, 2010 by Life Sentence Publishing, Inc. • Quotations from the Wycliffe Bible Copyright © 2000 by Terence P. Noble. • Quotations from the International Standard Version (ISV) Copyright © 1995–2014 by ISV Foundation. All rights reserved internationally. • Quotations from The Names of God Bible (NOG) © 2011 by Baker Publishing Group. • The New Jerusalem Bible (NJB) © 1985 by Darton, Longman & Todd Ltd and Doubleday, a division of Bantam Doubleday Dell Publishing Group, Inc. • Scripture quotations from The Revised Standard Version of the Bible, copyright © 1946, 1952, 1971 by the Division of Christian Education of the National Council of the Churches of Christ in the United States of America. Used by permission. All rights reserved.

p. 186: Extract taken from the song 'May the fragrance of Jesus fill this place' by Graham Kendrick. Copyright © 1986 Thankyou Music. Used with permission.

Every effort has been made to trace and contact copyright owners for material used in this resource. We apologise for any inadvertent omissions or errors, and would ask those concerned to contact us so that full acknowledgement can be made in the future.

A catalogue record for this book is available from the British Library

Printed and bound in Great Britain by Clays Ltd, Elcograf S.p.A.

Sensing the
Divine

John's word made flesh

Andrew D. Mayes

Contents

Introduction

The city was frenetic, throbbing, pulsating below him, and John's pen hovered over the parchment. Dare he write it? Dare he put into ink the four most outrageous words ever written, that *would* ever be written? Words that are either utter madness or life-transforming truth?

As John looked out over the city, he witnessed a heaving metropolis, a vibrant centre of commerce humming with human life and bristling with unstoppable energy. He viewed the buzzing harbour and docks, ships unburdening themselves of varied cargo. All life was there, in Ephesus. Prostitution was rife, some associated with the temple to Diana, Artemis the fertility deity, her sanctuary hailed as one of the seven wonders of the ancient world. It was precisely in this social setting, this urban context, that he penned words that would change the world: 'The Word became flesh.' In Ephesus, the very word 'flesh' took on a meaning that was visceral, earthy, full of passion.

The original inspiration for this book comes from reading the prologue to John's gospel in its most probable original setting. As course director of St George's College, Jerusalem, I led pilgrimages not only throughout the Holy Land – celebrated in two other books[1] – but also in Turkey, ancient Asia Minor. A highlight of such a tour is Ephesus, magnificently excavated to reveal its Roman treasures, many dating from the time of Hadrian but significant elements from the time of Christ.

John in Ephesus

Irenaeus (d. 202), in his work *Against Heresies*, written about 185, affirms that the author of the fourth gospel was John the Lord's disciple, who wrote it at Ephesus, where John remained until the time of Trajan. Eusebius tells us that Irenaeus' authority for these statements was Polycarp, who learned truth from the apostles. Polycarp taught Irenaeus, passing on to him stories about John.[2]

Irenaeus relates how Polycarp told him this episode:

> John, the disciple of the Lord, going to bathe at Ephesus, and seeing Cerinthus [the gnostic] inside, rushed out of the bath-house without bathing, exclaiming, 'Let us fly, in case even the bath-house fall down, because Cerinthus, the enemy of the truth, is inside.'[3]

This vignette is not only part of the chain of testimony linking these early Christian generations, but it also supplies a minor clue about the opulence and luxury of Ephesus at this time.

Appreciating creation

As John looked out from his writing desk, he surveyed the horizons. In Roman times, Ephesus was situated on the northern slopes of the hills Coressus and Pion, and the dawn was breaking in the east, dispelling the gloom of night. The first rays of light were illuminating the hills. He glimpsed the turquoise Aegean Sea and enjoyed watching the unceasing movement of the incoming waves. His eyes alighted on the ribbon of the river Cayster, and the stunning Meander Valley. He was awestruck by the mountains that surrounded him, with their exposed rocks and cover of cypress trees. He looked down on the vineyards below, and the irrigated horticulture with its rich harvest of fruits of every kind. Looking up, he saw the bluest of skies, broken only by the occasional cloud. He felt the wind blowing on his face, rustling his parchments. As he surveyed the creation around him, below him and above him, he began to write:

> In the beginning was the Word, and the Word was with God, and the Word was God. He was in the beginning with God. All

things came into being through him, and without him not one thing came into being. What has come into being in him was life, and the life was the light of all people. The light shines in the darkness, and the darkness did not overcome it... He was in the world, and the world came into being through him.

JOHN 1:1–5, 10

John's timeless words were not written in a vacuum. They are not an abstract philosophical treatise. They are a hymn of praise, a poem that springs from a certain context. They refer to an environment, an ecology, that John saw with his own enquiring eyes. John will go on in his gospel to delight in the natural world, because he sees Jesus the Word in every wave and every fold in the hills, in every leaf and bud. He will go on to see how the vine, the flowing water, the seed, the shepherd and the lamb reveal God the Word. For John, the Word – the very instrument and tool by which God originated and shaped the cosmos – has focused its divine power and presence in the human life of Jesus.

Celebrating incarnation

When John was in Ephesus, its sprawling population numbered about 150,000. It was the one of the largest cities of the Roman empire, a pivotal trade and administrative centre, as well as a focus of pilgrimage to Artemis. It enjoyed a rich and sensuous culture. It boasted a theatre, seating 25,000 spectators, mentioned in the Acts of the Apostles (19:29), and a significant stadium. The city had a number of temples, testifying to the multicultural and pluralistic nature of its society. Statues of the healing god Asclepius, Aphrodite, Dionysus, Hygeia and Pan were found in the bath-gymnasium complex – a place not only for cleansing and healing, but for sport and sexual activities of all orientations. The brothels of the city were infamous and much frequented.

As a key crossroads of civilisation, politically Ephesus was hailed as 'the supreme metropolis of Asia'. The Roman governor of the region lived there. Economically, Ephesus was a giant among first-century cities. With its strategic location, it was the chief commercial centre of western Asia Minor. Its harbour welcomed ships from around the Mediterranean and even from India, while its two major roads gave ready access to other cities along the coast and inland. A city used to welcoming foreign guests, travellers and traders, a variety of ethnicities and races were represented in its populace.

In Ephesus, it could be rightly said, 'All human life was there': traders and sailors, craftsmen and artisans, priests and prostitutes, sages and shopkeepers. Poverty and need coexisted with opulence and riches. The population was swelling: those 'who were born... of blood or of the will of the flesh or of the will of man' (John 1:13). Ephesus was an important centre of the slave trade, with men and women bought and sold to be used in mining, construction or domestic settings. Indeed, a quarter of the city's population was composed of slaves. The city's wealth was underpinned by the untold, underground story of slavery and exploitation.

As John looked out on this multifaceted mosaic of human life, he drew a deep breath. His pen hovered for a moment above the page. Dare he commit to writing those words that had been drumming in his mind, as he tried to encapsulate the mystery of Jesus? Was it too much to affirm? As he looked at the city below him, with its blend of sweat and fragrance, its maelstrom of human emotion and fleshly activity, his pen touched the parchment. There was no going back:

> And the Word became flesh and lived among us, and we have seen his glory, the glory as of a father's only son, full of grace and truth... From his fullness we have all received, grace upon grace.
> JOHN 1:14, 16

These words in the prologue to John's gospel – celebrating creation and incarnation, Word and flesh – announce to the reader what is to come. John knows that he is pondering a paradox. The one of whom he will write is at once 'from above' yet living fully here below. John will need to combine, somehow, the intimacy and ultimacy of Jesus, his transcendence and tenderness. His testimony will be at once sublime and visceral. Later, he will write in a letter:

> We declare to you what was from the beginning, what we have heard, what we have seen with our eyes, what we have looked at and touched with our hands, concerning the word of life – this life was revealed, and we have seen it and testify to it, and declare to you the eternal life that was with the Father and was revealed to us – we declare to you what we have seen and heard so that you also may have fellowship with us; and truly our fellowship is with the Father and with his Son Jesus Christ. We are writing these things so that our joy may be complete.
> 1 JOHN 1:1–4

While in Palestine, John had seen for himself with his own eyes and touched for himself with his very hands the mystery of Jesus. Now he longs with all his heart not only to communicate his discovery to others, but also to invite them, in some sense, to reach out and encounter Jesus. He has no alternative. If he is writing of a sensual Christ, of flesh that bears the Word, he must write a sensual gospel.[4]

For John, the person of Jesus is an intriguing enigma and paradox. He is 'from above' – a transcendent figure, the divine Son of God. Yet he is also earthly, and reveals human vulnerabilities: thirsting, hungry, fatigued. The Jesus of the fourth gospel delights in human company, relationships, touch and physical contact.

Infinity meets fragility, transcendence blends with tenderness, meekness radiates majesty. The prologue gives us a glimpse of the intimacy between Father and Son: 'No one has ever seen God. It is God the only Son, who is close to the Father's heart, who has made him known' (1:18). Actually, John refers to Jesus' being 'in the Father's bosom [Greek: *kolpon*]'. This word is repeated when he writes of the beloved disciple at the last supper reclining 'in the bosom of Jesus' (13:23). The intimacy between Father and Son is mirrored in the relationship of Jesus and disciple. Indeed, Jesus describes friendship in terms of a sharing of secrets: 'I have called you friends, because I have made known to you everything that I have heard from my Father' (15:15). In the same discourse, pouring water intimately over the bare feet of the disciples, Jesus says: 'I have set you an example, that you also should do as I have done' (13:15). Jesus' sensuality and experience of intimacy is paradigmatic – in it, he offers us an ideal to emulate.

Spiritual gospel?

Since the earliest times, the fourth gospel has often been character-ised by commentators and writers as the most mystical of the gospels. Cyril of Alexandria (378–444) hailed John's work as 'the spiritual gospel'.[5] This labelling stuck and encouraged a symbolic reading of the text, a search for an esoteric Johannine mysticism.[6] Cyril was contrasting it with the other gospels, which had recorded, he felt, the 'bodily facts' of Jesus' life and ministry. John was doing something different, he thought, by placing an emphasis on the symbolic over against the physical.

In his *Commentary on the Gospel of John*, Origen (185–254) writes:

> What John calls the eternal gospel, and what may properly be called the spiritual gospel, presents clearly to those who have the will to understand, all matters concerning the very Son of God, both the mysteries presented by His discourses and those matters of which His acts were the enigmas.[7]

In the fourth century, Augustine of Hippo wrote:

> In the four gospels, or rather in the four books that make up the one gospel, it was St John who in his teaching soared to heights far loftier than those attained by the other three

evangelists, and it was his wish to carry our hearts with him on his flight. The other three walked with the Lord as with a man upon the earth and said little concerning his divinity. But John, as though scorning to tread upon earth, rose by his very first words not only above the earth, above the atmosphere, above the heavens, but even above the whole army of angels and all the array of invisible powers. The sublimity of this beginning was well matched by all that followed, for John spoke of the divinity of our Lord as no other has ever spoken.[8]

Augustine likens John to the eagle who can soar higher than any other bird, because John's 'spiritual understanding compared to the eagle, has elevated his preaching higher, and far more sublimely, than the other three'.[9] In this passage, Augustine suggests that the author of the fourth gospel is not only elevated but his feet are not on the ground; he is soaring above the earth.

Aim of this book

It is the contention of this book that the fourth gospel is rooted in the dust, dirt and beauty of the earth. It brims with sensuality, alerting and activating our senses, both bodily and spiritual. It is pervaded by a physicality, a materiality, shot through with transcendence, teeming with divine life. This book aims to do three things. First, we shall appreciate afresh the meaning and significance of the most outrageous of all Christian claims: the idea that the divine Word took flesh in Jesus of Nazareth. We will trace this theme through the fourth gospel, identifying and celebrating its sensuous, tactile character. Second, we shall see what implications this has for the practice of Christian spirituality, and what this suggests for contemporary ways of praying and acting. The gospel of John will be a springboard, a catalyst, a stimulus as we search for forms of spirituality that speak to us today and connect with people's contemporary search for the divine. Third, we shall conclude by pondering its significance for the nature of mission in today's world.

Approach of this book

In this book, we will enjoy exploring the ways in which the fourth gospel combines spirituality and physicality. As we ponder the themes, we will also be on the lookout for clues to a spirituality relevant to our own time and clues about our contemporary mission in the world. The book can be used in groups, and both questions for reflection and practical directions for prayer exercises are offered at the end of each chapter.

This is a book for enquirers and those seeking a spiritual way today. It is a resource for teachers and preachers. It can well be used by spiritual directors and by retreat-givers – indeed, the contents of this book suggest a rich outline for a retreat or an agenda for various sessions with a parish group or prayer group.

As we look at the senses in the fourth gospel, we will discover that John has a singular approach to each of them, quite unlike the other gospels. He approaches the senses in a unique and distinctive way and gives to them a particular meaning: looking, listening, touching, tasting, drinking and eating, and even scent has a singular meaning. This is not incidental or accidental, but springs from John's conviction: 'The Word was made flesh.' For John, the senses have a deep theological significance, challenging and inspiring the practice of spirituality today and pertinent to the very nature of our engagement with the world.

The need for this book

We need to rediscover a sensuous gospel today, because for centuries the Christian religion has been plagued by a dualism between flesh and spirit that has led it to be dehumanising.

The formative first centuries of the church were infected by Neoplatonism. Monastic life, which developed as the paradigm of

Christian perfection, celibacy and hatred of the body, maintained by all forms of self-mortification, forced Christianity into the mould of a world-denying not world-affirming faith. Divisive, dualistic thinking gave rise to disastrous polarities in Christian thinking, as things were pitched against one another. Heaven was opposed to earth, the body to the spirit. Politics and prayer were to be kept separate. Sacred and secular were delineated with barriers, as if they were two separate realms, holy and unholy. The church and the world are set against each other. There is a natural human tendency towards polarisation, keeping things apart. It has to do with being in control, trying to make sense of things neatly, seeing things in black and white, but as we know it can lead to fundamentalism, racism, homophobia, fear of the other. We feel safer when we oppose, judge, differentiate, label and compare.

Today, we live in a polarised world: Republican vs Democrat, Conservative vs Labour, Protestant vs Catholic, east vs west. Things are often said to be black or white. In the UK, Parliament is based on government and opposition being locked in perpetual combat. We are uneasy with the idea of coalition; we say: 'It shouldn't be like this! It will never work!' Bifurcation is the preferred option. It has been said, we live in a 'tit-for-tat universe'.[10] Binary operating is not only confined to the workings of the computer; it infects our very mindset. In spirituality, dualistic thinking has created unnecessary distances and opened up uncalled-for chasms. Where God is thought of as something 'out there' or 'up there', the divine is perceived to be remote and unapproachable.

But John does not tolerate such a dualism. While 'no one has ever seen God', he delights that the divine is indeed seen and felt in the person of Jesus. For him, the two worlds meet in Jesus: they intersect, they interpenetrate. The Word became flesh. The incarnation is a breakthrough.

But there is another reason why this study is timely. In today's culture, we are increasingly removed from the natural world.

Technology is distancing us from nature, keeping us at one remove, at least, from an immediacy of contact and touch with the physical world. We have inserted a range of electronic gadgetry between ourselves and our environs and, while this might have the potential to be a lens, a magnifying glass as it were, it often turns out to be a barrier that fences us off from the natural world. This journey through John's gospel will help us to reconnect with the ground beneath our feet. It will stimulate a re-engagement, a re-enchantment with God's world, which is brimming with epiphanies. John will help us to recognise and welcome these, to rediscover theophany. He will help us, indeed, to become fully human once again, activating afresh our senses and sensibilities.

In this book, each chapter is in two parts as we explore this theme. First, we discover how John invites us to open our eyes, unstop our ears and discover God through one of the senses. In the second part of each chapter, we seek to retrieve from the Christian tradition examples of how Christian spirituality celebrates the use of such senses in the practice of prayer and in the outworking of our faith.

An invitation to respond

The reader-response approach to literature has alerted us to the vital role that the reader enjoys when interacting with the written text: the experience of the reader meets the givenness of the written word in a unique dynamic that unlocks fresh possibilities for appreciation of the work. The fourth gospel invites us into such an exploratory relationship. We are summoned to engage with the text with body, mind and soul. This can be an unpredictable exercise: we need to be ready to be surprised, shocked, disturbed, heartened, moved and challenged by our encounter with John's gospel. Our physical and spiritual senses can be stimulated and reactivated. We need to be prepared for a fresh reading that may change and transform us in the process. Culpepper pioneered such an approach to the gospel by his attentiveness to time, plot and characterisation within the narrative.[11] Staley took this further in his study *The Print's First Kiss*.[12] This present book asks of its reader an openness, a readiness to respond, a preparedness to receive the impact of God's word afresh. This book is not a literary analysis of the fourth gospel but a springboard for prayer, reflection and deeper engagement with God's world.

Overview

The first two chapters open up the journey for us. We begin our encounter with the fourth gospel by taking a look at the physicality of Christ and the use of our bodily and spiritual senses. Second, we seek to activate our 'sixth sense' and explore how John's gospel summons us into a deeper kind of knowing. Our journey gets underway as in chapters 3 and 4 we appreciate the acute sense of place and time in the fourth gospel. Successive chapters take us through the senses: the theme of touch and feel (chapter 5) enables us to explore both the physicality and the emotionality of Jesus in the gospel. After engaging with the key senses of sight (chapter 6) and hearing (chapter 7), we look at the less appreciated themes of taste (chapter 8) and scent (chapter 9). We conclude by celebrating how John's gospel summons us to life in all its fullness – to becoming fully alive and awake to God's revelations and epiphanies, however they may come (chapter 10). It is hoped that this book will be empowering and liberating for you as you unfold the sensuous gospel!

1

Unleashing the senses: the Word made flesh

We are being invited to enjoy the gospel of John as a sensual gospel. It is literally *sensational*, brimming and overflowing with tangible signs. It summons us to unexpected perceptions and knowledge through the senses. It calls us to discover a new *sensibility* – a fresh openness, and indeed vulnerability; a susceptibility to receiving insights and experiences through the senses. John's readers are *sentient beings*, capable of perceiving and feeling a diversity of impressions. The gospel challenges us to new *sensitivity* as we read the text – an awareness, a heightened sense of anticipation, a readiness to receive God's stunning self-revelation to us. This gives us a hermeneutical key – a lens through which to enjoy the fourth gospel and the world around us afresh. Let us return to our senses!

We will discover the fourth gospel to be at once visceral and mystical. It celebrates both the mortality and the transcendence of Christ, his power and his gentleness. Paradoxically, at the same time we encounter in the person of Jesus nobility and tenderness, strength and vulnerability, glory and suffering, humanity and divinity, meekness and majesty, manhood and deity, power and fragility. The divine has real human blood flowing through his veins. Throughout this book, we will see how the fourth gospel calls us to deification not mortification, to transfiguration of the flesh not its subjugation. We will see how it invites us to discover a spirituality that is integral to our humanity, integrated with our physicality, embodied. The kind of spirituality that the fourth gospel encourages is grounded, earthed yet open to theophany in unexpected places and people.

In this opening chapter, first we explore key concepts in the prologue of John's gospel, especially the Word and the flesh. We take an overview of the times that John points us to the physical body of Jesus. In the second part of the chapter, we discover a diverse range of spiritualities that open for us an encounter with the divine through the senses. We look at the idea of spiritual senses: inner faculties for perceiving the divine, related to outward senses. We look at devotion to the sacred humanity of Jesus, expressed in devotion to the Passion and in bridal mysticism.

The Word was made flesh

'The Word'

Taking a fresh look at the prologue to the gospel, we realise how it stands as a preface alerting us to what is to come. Scholars have long debated the background to John's use of *Logos*, the Word. What does John wish us to keep in mind as he writes of the role of the Word in the creation of the world, the Word that in the fullness of time will be enfleshed and embodied in the person of Jesus? Some point to the Greek background – and this emphasises the solemn and serious import of the word *Logos* – which represents the rational principle, ensuring order and stability in creation. In Stoic philosophy, *Logos* connotes the structuring principle of the universe, a formal abstraction behind created reality. Greek philosophers such as Philo thought of the *Logos* as representing divine reason and logic, bringing order into the midst of chaos. It is a staid and stolid approach.

But the Hebrew background evokes joyful, frisky, gambolling playfulness in the heart of God. The *Logos* in the Hebrew scriptures represents God's playmate in the act of creation, God's *Sophia* or wisdom, as Proverbs 8 puts it:

The Lord created me at the beginning of his work,
    the first of his acts of long ago.
Ages ago I was set up,
    at the first, before the beginning of the earth.
When there were no depths I was brought forth,
    when there were no springs abounding with water.
Before the mountains had been shaped,
    before the hills, I was brought forth –
when he had not yet made earth and fields,
    or the world's first bits of soil.
When he established the heavens, I was there,
    when he drew a circle on the face of the deep,
when he made firm the skies above,
    when he established the fountains of the deep,
when he assigned to the sea its limit,
    so that the waters might not transgress his command,
when he marked out the foundations of the earth,
    then I was beside him, like a master worker
and I was daily his delight,
    rejoicing before him always,
rejoicing in his inhabited world
    and delighting in the human race.
PROVERBS 8:22–31

A Jewish translation[1] gives us (vv. 30–31):

And I was daily all delight,
    Playing always before Him,
Playing in His habitable earth.

The New Century Version gives us (v. 30):

I was like a child by his side.
I was delighted every day,
    enjoying his presence all the time.

The Message translates the last verse:

> Day after day I was there, with my joyful applause,
>   always enjoying his company.

This is a dynamic and vibrant view of the *Logos*: the one who is rejoicing in the playfulness of creation, as a little child delights in making new things, crafting and shaping materials. Such an energy, a verve, a daring, a passionate life force, a sparkling vitality – this is now to be embodied in the person of Jesus.

'He was in the world'

'He was in the world, and the world came into being through him; yet the world did not know him' (1:10). These verses are often taken to refer to the coming of Jesus of Nazareth, his advent in the land of Palestine as an historical event and his rejection by the people of Israel. However, they are given to us before reference is made by the author to the incarnation in verse 14 and so refer to the homecoming of the Word in creation itself, not to incarnation. We are being invited to see the very creation, the natural world, as the embodiment of the divine presence: 'He was in the world.' The prologue sets this theme before us in order to alert us to the discovery we may make of the divine Word in the natural world as the gospel of John unfolds before us. He has already told us that 'all things came into being through him, and without him not one thing came into being' (1:3). We are being called to recognise that the divine Word is to be encountered from molecule to galaxy, from dust to mountain.

'Made flesh'

First, we should note that the Greek word *sarx*, which we translate as 'flesh', can be wider in its connotations than the human body. The Word in Jesus is in solidarity with all created things. Gregersen has written of 'deep incarnation', by which he means that the Word made flesh is conjoined and united with created matter throughout the universe, with all living beings.[2] Elizabeth Johnson puts it:

> In becoming flesh, the Word/Wisdom of God lays hold of matter in the form of a human being… The *sarx* of Jesus of Nazareth was a complex unit of minerals and fluids, an item in the carbon, oxygen and nitrogen cycles, a moment in the biological evolution of this planet. The atoms comprising his body were once part of other creatures. The genetic structure of his cells made him kin to the grasses, the fish, the whole community of life that descended from common ancestors in the ancient seas. Like all human beings, Jesus carried with himself [as Sean McDonagh puts it] 'the signature of the supernovas and the geology and life history of the Earth'. The *sarx* of John 1:14 thus reaches beyond the person of Jesus and beyond all other human beings to encompass the whole biological world of living creatures and the cosmic dust of which they are composed. In this perspective, the flesh that the Word/Wisdom of God became is part of the vast body of the cosmos.[3]

John's gospel displays an attentiveness to the flesh of Jesus and indeed to all human flesh, so that Dorothy Lee can affirm:

> For John, the role of flesh in salvation is neither arbitrary nor incidental, but essential. It is the core Johannine symbol of salvation, in which the material realm becomes the bearer of divine reality… The flesh of Jesus is not an evanescent or fanciful symbol… It becomes the core symbol of the gospel.[4]

Encountering the body of Jesus

Let us see how frequently John directs us to the physicality and tangible reality of Jesus' own flesh and body.

In his ministry

- In chapter 1, John relates how Jesus passed through the waters of the Jordan in his baptism. He alludes to the feet of Jesus in reference to his sandals.
- In chapter 2, Jesus exerts himself physically in overturning tables and driving animals from the temple precincts. He speaks of 'the temple of his body'. Later, he joins a village wedding, and his mouth enjoys its lavish refreshments.
- In chapter 3, Jesus speaks about childbirth.
- In chapter 4, we see that Jesus is wearied and tired after his journey, with sweat on his brow; he thirsts and he is hungry.
- In chapters 5 and 9, Jesus walks through the streets of Jerusalem.
- In chapter 6, Jesus takes seriously the hungering of the crowd.
- In chapter 7, Jesus refers to the physical act of circumcision.
- In chapter 8, his fingers mark a sign in the dust of the ground.
- In chapter 9, his mouth emits spittle, to be made into a healing paste. With this, he touches the closed eyes of the man born blind.
- In chapter 10, Jesus shelters from the cold winter weather in the covered Porch of Solomon.
- In chapter 11, tears course down Jesus' face: he weeps at the tomb of Lazarus. He is anguished and distressed.
- In chapter 12, his feet are anointed by Mary at Bethany, as she pours fragrant perfume over them, a sign preparing for the burial to come.
- In chapter 13, Jesus' hands minister to the feet of the disciples in the foot-washing.

In his Passion

The Passion narratives give particular attention to the wounded body of Jesus. This directs us to take seriously the very human body of Jesus, and to gaze upon its different parts:

- His breast invites the presence of the beloved disciple at the last supper (13:23).

- His fingers dip the bread at the last supper (13:26).
- His head is crowned with thorns (19:2). His head is bowed in death (19:30).
- His lips crave: 'I thirst!' (19:28). Lips that once had supped the wine of Cana and given spittle to the blind man now on the cross take a drought of vinegar, moistening them, quenching his raging thirst. 'A jar full of sour wine was standing there. So they put a sponge full of the wine on a branch of hyssop and held it to his mouth' (19:29). In a reference to his Passion, Jesus asks: 'Shall I not drink the cup which the Father has given me?' (18:11).
- His breath is exhaled upon fearful disciples: 'He breathed on them' (20:22).
- His shoulders bear the weight of the cross (19:17).
- His back is furrowed by scourging (19:1).
- Soldiers are authorised to break his legs, if necessary (19:32–33).
- His side is pierced with a spear (19:34).
- His blood oozes from the wounds inflicted (19:34).
- His physical body is mentioned four times (19:38–40; 20:12). It is clothed with a purple robe (19:5), stripped naked by the soldiers (19:23) and wrapped in linen cloths (19:40; 20:5–7).
- His hands will be examined by the disciples and by Thomas (20:20, 27).

As Pilate declares: 'Behold the man!' (19:5); 'Here he is: the Man!' (MSG). This is no spiritualised gospel; it is a physical gospel. Jesus is tangible, palpable, visceral, material. Why does John emphasise this?

Double trouble

At the time of his writing, the infant church was plagued by two heresies.

Docetism (from *dókēsis*, meaning 'apparition', 'phantom') began to flourish as people could not come to terms with the scandal and outrage of the incarnation: writers such as Marcion (85–160) attempted to rationalise it. Jesus' body must have been either absent or illusory. It only seemed to be human, and his human form was an apparition. Christ was so divine he could not have been human, since God lacked a material body, which therefore could not physically suffer. Jesus only appeared to be a flesh-and-blood man, when really he was divine. In this view, Jesus is seen as God simply pretending, or play-acting, at being human, because it was held that divinity and humanity are absolutely incompatible, and there was no way that divine life was going to be contaminated by a human body.

The other heresy beginning to develop was Gnosticism, which we will look at in the next chapter: the belief that all matter is evil and the body is a prison from which we need to escape. Gnosticism would want to see Jesus as a wisdom teacher of secret *gnosis* or knowledge. In their view, Christ did not really suffer on the cross. He is not really a man, but a demigod.

So John is empathic. He directs our gaze to the real body of Jesus in the Passion. Human, red blood and haemoglobin course through his veins. John's main conviction is that the Word – the divine Word, through whom God created the universe – became flesh and dwelt among us. For, in the fourth gospel, Jesus is neither just a holy teacher nor an apparition; he is God in flesh and blood, God in a human form, God among us. In his gospel, John will tell us that this dusty God thirsts. He weeps. He bleeds. He dies. He shares our human condition completely, utterly.

Thomas is insistent: 'Unless I see the mark of the nails in his hands, and put my finger in the mark of the nails and my hand in his side, I will not believe' (20:25). And to Thomas, the risen Christ will say, in the days after Easter: 'Put your finger here and see my hands. Reach out your hand and put it in my side. Do not doubt but believe.' Thomas will answer him: 'My Lord and my God!' (20:27–28). It is by encountering the real body and physicality of Jesus that he will come to faith.

'We have seen his glory': glory in the midst of physicality

The dominant theme of the fourth gospel is glory bubbling up in 'signs', in the midst of human flesh and blood. What is 'glory' in John's perspective? It is the visible radiance of the divine presence – a sign that God is powerfully at work. John introduces this key theme in his words: 'And the Word became flesh and lived among us, and we have seen his glory, the glory as of a father's only son, full of grace and truth' (1:14). How is this glory to be revealed? God's glory is manifested through 'signs' that in human flesh reveal divine transformations and celebrate a new creation unfolding:

1   Changing water into wine (2:1–11) – 'the first of his signs'
2   Healing the royal official's son in Capernaum (4:46–54)
3   Healing the paralytic at Bethesda (5:1–15)
4   Feeding the 5,000 (6:5–14) and Jesus' walk on water (6:16–24)
5   Healing the man born blind (9:1–7)
6   The raising of Lazarus (11:1–45)

The crucifixion is seen as the culminating seventh sign. Divine glory is supremely and paradoxically to be revealed in the physicality of the cross, the greatest moment of God's revelation, the laying bare of his presence, as we shall explore in chapter 6.

. . . .

Spirituality of the senses

Activating the spiritual senses

While the Hebrew scriptures declare that creation is 'very good', the Christian faith affirms that the divine Word became enfleshed, embodied, taking on human flesh and blood in the person of Jesus Christ. In the wake of the incarnation, physicality and spirituality become inseparable.

Ephrem the Syrian in the fourth century exults:

> *Let us see those things that He does for us every day!*
> *How many tastes for the mouth!*
> *How many beauties for the eye!*
> *How many melodies for the ear!*
> *How many scents for the nostrils!*
> *Who is sufficient in comparison*
> *To the goodness of these little things?*
> *Hymns on Virginity*, 31:16[5]

Gregory of Nyssa in the fourth century, in his commentary on the Song of Songs, describes the spiritual senses:

> We have two sets of senses, one corporeal and the other spiritual, as the Word tells us in the book of Proverbs: 'Thou shalt find the sense of God.' There is a correspondence between the motions and movements of the soul and the sense organs of the body... A kiss is an operation of the sense of touch: in a kiss, two pairs of lips touch. There is, however, a spiritual faculty of touch, which comes in contact with the Word, and this is actuated by a spiritual and immaterial sense of touch, as it is said: 'Our hands have handled of the word of life' (1 John 1:1).[6]

Augustine in his *Confessions* prays:

> Late have I loved you, beauty so old and so new: Late have I loved you. And see, you were within and I was in the external world and sought you there, and in my unlovely state I plunged into those lovely created things which you have made... You called and cried out loud and shattered my deafness. You were radiant and resplendent, you put to flight my blindness. You were fragrant, and I drew in my breath and now pant after you. I tasted you, and I feel but hunger and thirst for you. You touched me, and I am set on fire to attain the peace which is yours.[7]

In his autobiography, Jürgen Moltmann offers a contrasting prayer:

> For a long time, I looked for you within myself and crept into the shell of my soul, shielding myself with an armour of inapproachability. But you were outside – outside myself – and enticed me out of the narrowness of my heart into the broad place of love for life. So I came out of myself and found my soul in my senses, and my own self in others.[8]

Hildegard of Bingen (1098–1179), abbess, poet, artist and musician, writes:

> Humans grasp and know everything in creation with their five senses. They love with their faces, taste with their lips, analyse by hearing, seek with the scent that pleases them, and act with the feeling that makes them happy... And in doing this they have God, the Creator of everything, as their model.[9]

Troubadour St Francis of Assisi, the first poet to compose in the Italian vernacular, invites us to recognise and celebrate the radical and essential interconnectedness of all things, displaying a remarkable kinship and sense of unity with creation in his 'Canticle of Creation'. He hails the sun as brother and the moon as sister; he greets Sister Water and Brother Wind; and in his ministry he approached the fearsome wolf of Gubbio as 'brother'. At the dawn of capitalism and a creeping consumerist approach to things – Francis was the son of a wealthy cloth merchant and worked in his shop – he discovered a deep connectedness to all things, which was honouring and non-exploitative. Franciscan prayer nurtures such an appreciative and respectful approach to the world of nature.[10] In particular, Francis invites us to enjoy and celebrate a reciprocity in relation to the created world, a solidarity with the earth. The 'things of nature' are not objects to be manipulated but rather subjects; they act on us, as we respond with physical and spiritual senses. As David Abram puts it:

> There is an intimate reciprocity to the senses; as we touch the bark of a tree, we feel the tree *touching us*; as we lend our ears to the local sounds and ally our nose to the seasonal scents, the terrain gradually tunes us in turn. The senses, that is, are the primary way that the earth has of informing our thoughts and of guiding our actions.[11]

Indeed, Francis' very conversion was effected by a physical embrace of a leper on the road outside Assisi. Normally, he recoiled at the sight of the disfigured and disabled sufferers; in fact, he had an absolute horror of them and would avoid going near their colonies at all costs. But something stirred within his heart when he met this tortured man in the lane, with bandaged hands and dressed in rags. He felt impelled, constrained by something within, not only to approach the man but to touch him tenderly, to embrace him with his own lips. Later, he wondered if he had not met Christ himself in this encounter. Poignantly, in his own words, Francis describes this as a turning point in his life:

> This is how God inspired me, Brother Francis, to embark upon a life of penance. When I was in sin, the sight of lepers nauseated me beyond measure; but then God himself led me into their company, and I had pity on them. When I had once become acquainted with them, what had previously nauseated me became a source of spiritual and physical consolation for me [lit.

'sweetness in soul and body']… We bless you, because by your holy cross you have redeemed the world.[12]

Francis found this tactile encounter an experience of radical conversion and transformation. In the very act of reaching out to someone and touching them, he was dramatically changed, never to be the same again. Later, his biographer Thomas of Celano wrote of him:

> So the spring of radiant love
> That filled his heart within
> Gushed forth.
> He was always with Jesus:
> Jesus in his heart,
> Jesus in his mouth,
> Jesus in his ears,
> Jesus in his eyes,
> Jesus in his hands,
> He bore Jesus always in his whole body.[13]

It was in solitude on Mount La Verna, praying for the grace to feel in his heart the intense love enkindled in Christ, that Francis received a particular embodiment of grace in the gift of the stigmata, receiving in his feet and hands, and in his side, an impression of the five wounds of the crucified Christ. This was the culmination of a life dedicated to penetrating the physicality and humanity of Jesus of Nazareth. For him, the words came literally true: 'I have been crucified with Christ; and it is no longer I who live, but it is Christ who lives in me. And the life I now live in the flesh I live by faith in the Son of God, who loved me and gave himself for me' (Galatians 2:19–20). Carretto puts it:

> When I realised that I had holes in my hands and feet, and especially that I had a wound in my side, I understood what it meant to live without trifling. Love is indeed a serious thing, a terrible challenge.[14]

Francis realised in that experience, at once intensely spiritual and searingly physical, that the Christian is invited to be fired, energised, empowered, transfigured, healed by such love.

Bonaventure, the Franciscan theologian of the 13th century, celebrates our discovery of God through senses, both physical and spiritual. First, we must activate our physical senses: 'Man [sic]... has five senses like five doors through which knowledge of all things which are in the sense world enters his soul.'[15] As we activate our senses, he says, we start to contemplate the world in all its tiniest detail and awesome vastness: the magnitude and size of things, the diversity of creation, its beauty, its order:

> Whoever, therefore, is not enlightened by such splendour of created things is blind; whoever is not awakened by such outcries is deaf; whoever does not praise God because of all these effects is dumb... Therefore, open your eyes, alert the ears of your spirit, open your lips and apply your heart so that in all creatures you may see, hear, praise, love and worship, glorify and honour your God.[16]

As we use our physical faculties of sense, says Bonaventure, something wonderful happens. We train ourselves to recognise the fingerprints of God, to trace the divine footprints in the soil – he calls these 'vestiges of God' – that help us recognise the divine power, the divine wisdom and the divine goodness in all things: 'In God alone there is primordial and true delight and... in all of our delights we are led to seek this delight.'[17] Our spiritual senses become triggered, activated, leading us into prayer:

> When the inner senses are restored to see the highest beauty, to hear the highest harmony, to smell the highest fragrance, to taste the highest sweetness, to apprehend the highest delight, the soul is prepared for spiritual ecstasy through devotion, admiration and exultation.'[18]

This is the invitation of prayer.

Julian of Norwich (1342–1416) has a deep appreciation of the physicality of the incarnation and has experienced in her body intimate touches of Christ. Her spirituality is embodied and enfleshed, and not at all abstract or theoretical but felt, experienced. When she writes of sensuality, she is referring to an experience of the senses, and a capacity to encounter the divine in bodily and emotional life:

> And when our soul is breathed into our body, at which time we are made sensual, at once mercy and grace begin to work… So I understood that our sensuality is founded on nature, in mercy and in grace, and this foundation enables us to receive gifts which lead us to endless life… I also saw that God is in our sensuality, for in the same instant and place in which our soul is made sensual, in that same instant and place exists the city of God, ordained for him from without beginning. He comes into this city and will never depart from it… That honourable city in which our Lord Jesus sits is our sensuality, in which he is enclosed.[19]

For Julian, body and soul form a 'glorious union'. This derives from the incarnation in which God himself takes on sensuality: 'Our sensuality is only in the second person, Christ Jesus.'[20] Julian invites us to experience God through the senses, which are at once a physical and a spiritual encounter:

> And so we shall by his sweet grace in our own meek continual prayer come into him now in this life by many secret touchings of sweet spiritual sights and feelings, measured out to us as our simplicity may bear it… We shall all be endlessly hidden in God, truly seeing and truly feeling, and hearing him spiritually and delectably smelling him and sweetly tasting him.[21]

Ignatius of Loyola, in the 16th century, invites us to hone our spiritual sensibilities: to activate our five senses within our imaginations vividly as we engage with the text, especially when we read the episodes from the life of Christ in the Bible. Ignatius says: Use your eyes to *look* at the scene, visualise it, imagine it in your mind's eye, place yourself into the picture and become one of the characters. Reach out in your imagination and *touch* with your fingertips the characters, the soil, the water, the physical aspects. Even *smell* the scents of the scene and *taste* the air, the food, the atmosphere. But above all, Ignatius says, open your ears and *listen* to what the characters are saying to each other, what they are saying to you and what God is saying to you through all this. This approach to scripture once again slows us down and demands time and attention. It leads to clearer discernment of God's will for us in the practice of ministry.[22]

Through such spiritual writers, we are being invited to develop in prayer a watchfulness, wakefulness, attentiveness, alertness. As we activate our spiritual senses, we start to live in new expectancy, on tiptoe as it were, ready to encounter the Word in anything and everything. We are ready for God's self-disclosures, and for God's surprises.

Devotion to the body of Jesus

Bridal mysticism
The fourth gospel places on the lips of John the Baptist: 'He who has the bride is the bridegroom. The friend of the bridegroom, who stands and hears him, rejoices greatly at the bridegroom's voice. For this reason my joy has been fulfilled' (3:29). Such imagery fanned the flames of an intensifying tradition of intimacy with Jesus the bridegroom, sometimes characterised as 'bridal mysticism'. This takes its inspiration from the Song of Songs in the Hebrew Bible.[23]

The Song celebrates the depths of a longing, passionate love. It not only uses erotic language, but it also develops the theme of hide and seek, the presence and absence of the lover, so the emotions of both communion and distress are explored. It moves from lines such as 'You have ravished my heart, my sister, my bride, you have ravished my heart with a glance of your eyes' (4:9) to 'I sought him, but did not find him; I called him, but he gave no answer' (5:6).

The Song of Songs became a rich inspiration for spiritual writers from Origen (third century) onwards: he began the long tradition of viewing this text as a description of the mystical relationship between Christ and the soul. Gregory of Nyssa (fourth century) approached the text through the lens of Neoplatonism and so was unable to appreciate the sheer physicality of the poems but felt the need to spiritualise and allegorise them.[24]

Through the centuries, spiritual writers have delighted in relational and social metaphors that enable them to explore the themes of spiritual dialogue, and intimacy with God. A key theme is *eros* as desire for God. This is explored by Augustine, who experiences for himself in the *Confessions* that 'our hearts will always be restless until they come to rest in God'. As Marilyn Sewell observes:

> The sacred is not in the sky, the place of transcendent, abstract principle, but rather is based on this earth, in the ordinary dwelling places of our lives, in our gardens and kitchens and bedrooms... and in our places of protest... The sacred is fuelled by *eros*, by desire. It is about passion. And compassion. And love. Always love.[25]

Bernard of Clairvaux (1090–1153) traces a certain progression as he preaches on the topic 'What it is to kiss the Lord's feet, hands and lips':

> This is the way and the order that must be followed. First, we fall at the feet of the Lord our Creator and lament our sins and faults. Second, we seek his helping hand to lift us up... Third... we may perhaps dare to lift up our eyes and view the Lord's glorious and majestic face. We are not only to adore him, but we are (and I say this with fear and trembling) to kiss him... made to be one Spirit in him.[26]

Richard of St Victor (died 1173) describes a 'steep stairway of love' with four stages in the relationship: betrothal, which corresponds with the stage of mystical purgation; courtship, which signifies mystical illumination; wedlock, the unitive stage; and the fruitfulness of conjugal relations, where the mystic bride becomes 'a parent of fresh spiritual life'. Richard 'saw clearly that the union of the soul with its Source could not be a barren ecstasy'.[27] The key in this narrative is the redirecting of erotic passion towards God, which includes sometimes vivid sexual, pregnancy and birthing imagery.

Meister Eckhart (13th century) writes, even more daringly than Richard, of giving birth to Christ from this naked immersion in Godhead – of the virgin becoming a wife to God and then of embodying and exuding the very compassion and justice of God, within which she is immersed in this most intimate union with God. He writes:

> From all eternity
> > God lies on a maternity bed
> > giving birth.
> The essence of God is birthing...
> And he asks:
> > What good is it to me
> > for the Creator to give birth to his/her son
> > if I do not also give birth to him
> > in my time
> > and my culture?[28]

The Beguines, in the 13th century, pioneered the use of erotic and sensual language to describe their relationship with divinity. The metaphors of lovemaking and intimacy not only embody the 'grammar of desire' and positive emotions, but such images can also be vehicles for negative feelings within the evolving relationship: a sense of failure, of disappointment or frustration, of puzzling absence as well as passionate presence. Hadewijch, a Dutch Beguine, sings of unrequited love:

He who lives on love with no success
Endures, in the madness of love,
Suffering that can only be known
By him who sincerely forsakes all for Love,
And then remains unnourished by her.
He is in woe because of Love;
For he sorely burns
In hope and in fear
Incessantly renewed.[29]

This finds its echoes even in the English tradition. John Donne (17th century) gives us in his work 'Batter my heart':

Take me to you, imprison me, for I
Except you enthral me, never shall be free,
Nor ever chaste, except you ravish me.[30]

He also prays: 'And let my amorous soul court thy mild Dove.'[31]

Thomas Traherne (1637–74) puts it:

He did approach, He did me woo;
I wonder that my God this thing would do.[32]

In hymns, too, we encounter this language. Charles Wesley sings: 'Jesus, lover of my soul, let me to thy bosom fly.' John Newton's hymn 'How sweet the name of Jesus sounds' includes the line 'Jesus! my Shepherd, Husband, Friend.' Nor is this limited to the west; it is universal. In the Orthodox liturgy of the eastern churches, Christ is often hailed as 'Thou lover of mankind'.

Devotion to the Passion

See from His head, His hands, His feet,
Sorrow and love flow mingled down!
Did e'er such love and sorrow meet,
Or thorns compose so rich a crown?

Isaac Watts' familiar hymn 'When I survey the wondrous cross' is but one example of entering into the mystery of the Passion by way of devotion to the sacred humanity of Christ. The Franciscan Father Andrew SDC (1869–1946) composed a popular hymn, 'O dearest Lord':

O dearest Lord, thy sacred head with thorns was pierced for me;
O pour thy blessing on my head that I may think for thee.
O dearest Lord, thy sacred hands with nails were pierced for me.
O shed thy blessing on my hands, that they may work for thee.
O dearest Lord, thy sacred feet with nails were pierced for me;
O pour thy blessing on my feet that they may follow thee.
O dearest Lord, thy sacred heart with spear was pierced for me;
O pour thy Spirit in my heart that I may live for thee.

Less familiar, but in the same vein, is the composition by Richard Crashaw (1613–49):

Lord, by this sweet and saving sign, defend us from our foes and
*   thine.*
Jesus, by thy wounded feet, direct our path aright.
Jesus, by thy nailed hands, move ours to deeds of love:
Jesus, by thy pierced side, cleanse our desires:
Jesus, by thy crown of thorns, annihilate our pride:
Jesus, by thy silence, shame our complaints:
Jesus, by thy parched lips, curb our cruel speech:
Jesus, by thy closing eyes, look on our sin no more:
Jesus, by thy broken heart, knit ours to thee.
And by this sweet and saving sign, Lord, draw us to our peace
*   and thine.*

Such devotional language goes back to the medieval hymn 'Salve caput cruentatum', which was originally attributed to Bernard of Clairvaux and probably dates from his era. It is addressed to the body of Christ hanging on the cross: to the feet, knees, hands, side, breast, heart and face. This inspired the much-loved hymn, sung to Bach's Passion Chorale, 'O sacred head now wounded':

> O sacred Head, now wounded, with grief and shame weighed down,
> Now scornfully surrounded with thorns, Thine only crown;
> O sacred Head, what glory, what bliss till now was Thine!
> Yet, though despised and gory, I joy to call Thee mine.
>
> What language shall I borrow to thank Thee, dearest friend,
> For this Thy dying sorrow, Thy pity without end?
> O make me Thine forever, and should I fainting be,
> Lord, let me never, never outlive my love for Thee.

What language, indeed, shall we borrow? John's gospel and the tradition of devotion to the sacred physicality of Christ, his humanity, vulnerability and woundedness, give us a starting point.

Recent writers summon us to wakefulness

Two recent writers open up for us fresh vistas of experience. Thomas Merton calls us to a high state of wakefulness:

> It might be a good thing to open our eyes and see. It is essential to experience all the times and moods of one good place.
> It is God's love that warms me in the sun and God's love that sends the cold rain. It is God's love that feeds me in the bread I eat and God's love that feeds me also by hunger and fasting... It is God who breathes on me with light winds off the river and in the breezes out of the wood...
> Everything we meet and everything we see and hear and touch... plants in us... something of heaven.

It is good and praiseworthy to look at some created thing and feel and appreciate its reality. Just to let the reality of what is real sink into you… for through real things we can reach Him who is infinitely real.[33]

More recently, David Steindl-Rast OSB invites us to encounter God through all the senses:

This is why wakefulness is so preeminent a task. How can I give a full response to this present moment unless I am alert to its message? And how can I be alert unless all my senses are wide awake? God's inexhaustible poetry comes to me in five languages: seeing, hearing, smelling, touching and tasting. All the rest is interpretation – literary criticism, as it were, not the poetry itself. Poetry resists translation. It can be fully experienced only in its original language. This is all the more true of the divine poetry of sensuousness. How then could I make sense of life if not through my senses?

We tend to overlook the close connection between responsiveness and responsibility, between sensuousness and social challenge. Outside and inside are of one piece. As we learn to really look with our eyes, we begin to look with our heart also. We begin to face what we might prefer to overlook, begin to see what is going on in this world of ours. As we learn to listen with our ears, our heart begins to hear the cry of the oppressed… We might sit down at table and taste the sweet and salty tears of the exploited which we import together with coffee and bananas. To be in touch with one's body is to be in touch with the world – that includes the Third World and all other areas with which our dull hearts are conveniently out of touch. No wonder that those in power, those interested in maintaining the status quo, look askance at anything that helps people come to their senses.[34]

• • • • • • • • • • • • • • • • • • •

Questions for reflection

1 How do you find yourself responding to the invitation of this chapter to encounter the divine in the physicality of Jesus' ministry and Passion? Are you intrigued, attracted or repelled?

2 What is your experience of the relationship between the physical and the spiritual senses?

3 Do you think that Docetism and Gnosticism have their modern-day counterparts? Where would you meet them?

4 How persistent do you feel is the body/soul dualism or dichotomy in today's practice of prayer? Have you noticed any changes in the last few years?

Prayer exercises

Get in touch with your body: awareness exercise

Imagine Jesus releasing over your head a generous portion of anointing oil. Feel it trickling down your body as the Holy Spirit invades every part of you. Recall Psalm 133:

How very good and pleasant it is
    when kindred live together in unity!
It is like the precious oil on the head,
    running down upon the beard,
on the beard of Aaron,
    running down over the collar of his robes.
It is like the dew of Hermon,
    which falls on the mountains of Zion.
For there the Lord ordained his blessing,
    life for evermore

Sense God's blessing resting on your head as a gentle weight. Feel it gently descend to your face and feel it over the surface of your skin, making your face radiant like Moses'.

Smile. Feel loved and cherished, valued and needed by God.

As you move to your chest, breathe in deeply and exhale, feeling the breath of God in your very lungs, literally inspiring you (the word 'inspire' comes from the Latin for 'blow into').

Permit the flow of blessing to descend to your stomach and loins. Allow God's blessing to flow down the length of your legs, to your feet.

End by thanking God that you are a veritable temple of the Holy Spirit (1 Corinthians 3:16). Pray in the words of the *Benedictus*: 'Guide our feet into the way of peace' (Luke 1:79). Be ready to go where God leads!

The Lord's Prayer using body

Our Father – *join hands*
In heaven – *raise high*
Hallowed be your name – *bow head*
Your kingdom come – *raise open hands in a gesture of invitation*
Your will be done – *make a salute*
On earth – *point hands down*
as it is in heaven – *lift hands and arms high above head*
Give us this day our daily bread – *open hands out ready to receive*
Forgive us our sins – *cross arms over chest*
as we forgive those who sin against us – *stretch arms out wide*
Lead us not into temptation but deliver us from evil – *place hands together over your face*
For yours is the kingdom, the power and the glory – *raise hands above head*
Forever and ever, Amen – *extend arms out wide, the body becoming cross-shaped*

Cross prayers of St Francis of Assisi

First, open your arms wide – extend them as far as you can. This embodies a solidarity with the cross. Think of Jesus opening wide his arms on the cross to embrace all who suffer, all who are in any form of distress. Think of Christ's all-encompassing love and acceptance.

Second, think of the risen Christ and the way he longs to enfold the whole of creation, the little ones and marginalised ones of the earth.

Third, offer this prayer as an act of intercession. It is a prayer that hurts – in the sense that your arms will grow weary and ache. Moses prayed like this and had to have others hold his arms up (Exodus 17:11–12). As you feel the ache, let it connect you to those who are in pain, those who are hurting: the sick, the dispossessed, those whose human rights are trampled on.

Finally, use this prayer as an act of self-offering. Offer yourself afresh to God for the part he has in store for you in his mission of reconciliation in the world.

2

Deep knowing:
a sense of the divine

For John, knowing is akin to a 'sixth sense'. In this chapter, we begin by noting the theme of searching for the divine in the fourth gospel. We see that, for John, knowing has a predominately Hebraic meaning, involving knowing with the heart, responding to God's revelations and epiphanies.

Humanity's quest for knowledge

The narrative of the fourth gospel opens with seekers, people searching. The very first words placed on the lips of Jesus are: 'What are you looking for?' (1:38); 'What seek ye?' (KJV). The opening chapter tells us about people who had an insatiable quest for knowledge: Andrew and his companion, Peter, Philip, Nathaniel... The fourth gospel recognises that the human spirit is thirsting for knowledge and the human mind is longing for answers. Who? What? Why? Where? How?

Who are you?

On several occasions, delegations from the religious elite initiate enquiry into Jesus. First, John the Baptist is investigated by agents of the Jerusalem establishment regarding both his identity and his relationship to Jesus (1:19–27). Later, the man cured of paralysis is questioned about Jesus (5:12–13), as are the parents of the man born blind (9:18–21). Jesus himself is asked specific questions about his identity: 'Who are you?' (8:25) and 'Who do you claim to be?' (8:53). Twice people ask him: 'Who is this Son of Man?' (9:35–36; 12:34).

What is this? What are you doing?

Pharisees ask the man born blind about Jesus: 'What do you say about him?' (9:17). Others ask Jesus: 'What sign are you going to give us?' (2:18; 6:30). Still others ask: 'What are we to do?' (6:28; 11:47). Knowledge about Jesus is sought: how he healed (9:26) or what crime he allegedly committed (18:29, 35). Twice it is asked: 'What does he mean?' (7:36; 16:17–18).

Why?

People ask 'Why?' questions: 'Why then are you baptising?' (1:25). 'Why listen to him?' (10:20). 'Why was this perfume not sold?' (12:5). 'Lord, why can I not follow you now?' (13:37).

Where?

A disciple asks Jesus: 'Where are you staying?' (1:38). Often there is complete mystification or ignorance about Jesus' true origins, and where he came from (6:41–42; 7:27–28). Similarly, people are left wondering about Jesus' destination – where he is heading: 'Where does this man intend to go?' (7:35). Sometimes the disciples dare not ask the 'Where?' question: 'But now I am going to him who sent me; yet none of you asks me, "Where are you going?"' (16:5).

How can this be? How can you say…?

Most frequently, humanity's quest for knowledge is revealed in the oft-recurring 'How?' question. 'How can anyone be born after having grown old?' (3:4). 'How can these things be?' (3:9). 'How can he now say, "I have come down from heaven"?' (6:42). 'How can this man give us his flesh to eat?' (6:52). 'How can you say that we shall be set free?' (8:33, NIV). 'How can you say that the Son of Man must be lifted up?' (12:34). 'How can we know the way?' (14:5). 'How is it that you will reveal yourself to us, and not to the world?' (14:22).

Knowing

'You will know the truth, and the truth will make you free' (8:32). In John, Jesus responds to this quest by speaking about knowing. John uses the word 'know' 109 times! John writes his gospel that we may come to believe and enter into the fullness of life (20:30–31). Barrett reminds us that 'knowledge is a vital theme of the gospel'.[1] It could almost to be said that 'knowing' represents a sixth sense in the fourth gospel – an awareness or intuition of the supernatural or divine. John would have known the famous text:

> The Lord created human beings out of earth,
>   and makes them return to it again...
> He endowed them with strength like his own,
>   and made them in his own image...
> They obtained the use of the five faculties of the Lord;
>   as sixth he distributed to them the gift of mind...
> Discretion and tongue and eyes,
>   ears and a mind for thinking he gave them.
> He filled them with knowledge and understanding...
> He bestowed knowledge upon them.
> ECCLESIASTICUS 17:1, 3, 5–7, 11

What did John have in mind when he talks about 'knowing'? What is the background to John's use of the word 'know'? Of course, there are various approaches to cognition and epistemology, but two from John's time stand out.

Plato's knowing

In John's time, Plato was popular, especially in Greek-speaking areas. For Plato, true knowledge comes from appreciation of the non-physical: by means of concepts, which he called Forms or Ideas. These belong to a higher, superior world above ours. This world is but a world of shadows (as in his 'allegory of the cave'). The way to this knowledge is by *theoria*, contemplation in the sense of intellectual abstract thinking – literally, being interested in the theoretical, ideological and philosophical. Plato's thought expressed a contrast between mind and body, spirit and flesh, the world above and the world below. His philosophy fostered a knowledge that reaches up to the real, eternal, changeless world above as this lower world was seen as ever-changing and passing away.

This is not what John had in mind!

Gnostic knowing

A second approach of his time is the proto-Gnosticism of the ancient world. Together with the mystery cults referred to in the New Testament (1 Timothy 6:20; Colossians 2:8), the Gnostics sought esoteric knowledge. They sought through initiation or illumination an acquisition of secret philosophical ideas. Their ideas were embodied in myths. Their quest for the divine involved increasing degrees of abstraction from this world, requiring repudiation of the body. Prominent was a dualism between a detested material world, considered inferior, and the exalted world of the spirit. They sought a redeemer from the spirit world to help them escape the material world and achieve enlightenment through participation in the spiritual realm. For the Gnostic, salvation lies in acquiring such knowledge, for our problem is not sin, needing atonement, but ignorance, needing knowledge. The texts found in Nag Hammadi in Egypt in the 1940s testify to how popular these ideas were in the second and third centuries. John Marsh writes:

> The Gnostic claims what saves is knowledge, knowledge of the origins of the world, of man in the world and of the way for man to escape from the world to union with God. But for John… the knowledge that will save is knowledge of the one true God,

and of Jesus Christ whom he has sent… The knowledge John would bring to men is not pure intellection; it is a response of mind and heart and will.[2]

This is not what John had in mind! So what *did* John have in mind when he wrote about knowing, and specifically knowing God?

Biblical knowing: the Hebrew view

The theme of knowing is introduced at the very beginning of Genesis with the tree of the knowledge of good and evil. The word 'know' (Hebrew: *yada*) is used to denote sexual intercourse: 'Now the man knew his wife Eve, and she conceived' (4:1). Knowledge comes through encounter and intimacy. Hunter reminds us that 'the Old Testament is an essential and pervasive element in St John's background. So full is his mind with its riches – words, ideas, types – that they become quite naturally vehicles for expressing his understanding of the new faith.'[3] Dodd is clear:

> While for the Greek knowledge of God is the most highly abstract form of pure contemplation, for the Hebrew it is essentially intercourse with God; it is to experience His dealings with men and women in time… [In the fourth gospel] we have therefore moved away from the Greek conception of knowledge in the direction of the Hebrew, from pure contemplation to experience, an experience in which God and humanity are in active intercourse.[4]

In Hebraic thought, knowing is dynamic. It is about engaging, entering into relationship, personally experiencing God's world. Knowing is about responding to the divine. Steeped in the Hebrew scriptures, John understands that the active use of the senses plays a vital role in the development of our relationships with others, the world and the divine. Hebrew scholar Yael Avrahami sums up the approach of the Old Testament:

The belief in divine creation of the senses, together with the emphasis on the embodied aspect of sensory experience, means that in ancient Israel carnal experience is a positive and important experience... Together, the different senses create a spectrum of meanings that completes the perceptive picture of the world, making the sensorium [sensory faculties] the main epistemological tool in biblical perception.[5]

This is what John had in mind!

Knowing with the head

Today, when talking about knowledge, we might make a contrast, for shorthand, between knowing with head or heart. To know with the head denotes academic know-how, intellectual knowledge, detached, rational, analytical mental reasoning. It requires a clever mind, a quick brain, an ability to grasp concepts, facts and figures. It is bookish and cerebral. This represents a certain approach to learning, focusing on the discursive, forming notions and deductions, utilising logic and reason. This could involve religious knowledge, concepts and knowledge *about* God – but it does not necessarily entail any knowledge *of* God.

It can be purely theoretical and impersonal – it does not require relationships. It can be gained in one's library or the study but not in the marketplace, home or street.

In the fourth gospel, we get examples of this. Martha says: 'I know that [my brother] will rise again in the resurrection on the last day' (11:24). She has grasped respectable orthodox Jewish belief and tenets of faith. She knows her religion and its creeds. But does she know God? The Jewish scribes know their stuff. They can say 'Abraham is our father' (8:39) and 'We know that God has spoken to Moses' (9:29). They have an intricate head knowledge of the Torah and of inherited dogma. Jesus challenges them: 'You search the scriptures because you think that in them you have eternal life... But

I know that you do not have the love of God in you' (5:39, 42). They thought they had got it 'up here', in the head, in the intellect; they did not get it in the heart.

Knowing with the heart

Foundational to Jewish experience is the daily repeated *Shema*:

> Hear, O Israel: The Lord is our God, the Lord alone. You shall love the Lord your God with all your heart, and with all your soul, and with all your might. Keep these words that I am commanding you today in your heart.
>
> DEUTERONOMY 6:4–6

To know with the heart – this is not sentimental or emotional. But it is holistic, discovering God at the very centre of our life, welcoming God at the core of our being, responding with all our God-given faculties and powers of understanding and will. This is a more intuitive approach, personally involving, engaging all our powers of perception and prayerful reflection.

In the Hebrew scriptures, the organ of knowledge is the heart: 'I will give them a heart to know that I am the Lord; and they shall be my people and I will be their God, for they shall return to me with their whole heart' (Jeremiah 24:7). The psalmist declares: 'My mouth shall speak wisdom; the meditation of my heart shall be understanding' (Psalm 49:3). As *The Catechism of the Catholic Church* reminds us:

> According to scripture, it is the *heart* that prays... The heart is the dwelling-place where I am, where I live; according to the Semitic or biblical expression, the heart is the place 'to which I withdraw'. The heart is our hidden centre... the place of encounter, because as image of God we live in relation.[6]

Pope Benedict XVI puts it: 'In biblical language, the heart (*Leb*) indicates the centre of human life, the point where reason, will, temperament and sensitivity converge, where the person finds his unity and his interior orientation.'[7] According to the Hebraic tradition, in which John stood, the heart is the very centre of the human, uniting the intellectual, emotional and volitional functions of the person.[8] It stands as a potent symbol of the inner life that is embodied and incarnate.

For John, it is the heart that matters. At the outset, John affirms: 'No one has ever seen God. It is God the only Son, who is close to the Father's heart, who has made him known' (1:18). Speaking exultantly of the gift of the Spirit, Jesus quotes the scripture: 'Out of the believer's heart shall flow rivers of living water' (7:38).

But he is saddened that hearts can be closed. Jesus quotes Isaiah: 'He has blinded their eyes and hardened their heart, so that they might not look with their eyes, and understand with their heart and turn – and I would heal them' (12:40; compare Isaiah 6:10). And John notes of the betrayal: 'The devil had already put it into the heart of Judas son of Simon Iscariot to betray him' (13:2). So Jesus finds it necessary to give this reassurance: 'Do not let your hearts be troubled' (14:1).

He observes: 'Sorrow has filled your hearts' (16:6) and goes on to offer hope of a new knowing: 'So you have pain now; but I will see you again, and your hearts will rejoice' (16:22).

Jesus himself models the sixth sense of knowing

Jesus knows humanity through and through. John is clear: 'But Jesus on his part would not entrust himself to them, because he knew all people and needed no one to testify about anyone; for he himself knew what was in everyone' (2:24–25). The Good Shepherd says: 'I know my own and my own know me, just as the Father knows me and I know the Father' (10:14–15). He seeks an answering knowledge: 'When he has brought out all his own, he goes ahead of them, and the sheep follow him because they know his voice. They will not follow a stranger, but they will run from him because they do not know the voice of strangers' (10:4–5).

In the fourth gospel, Jesus reads hearts. He knows that there is 'no deceit' in Nathanael (1:47) and that Peter 'loves him' (21:15–17). He can say penetratingly: 'You are looking for me, not because you saw signs, but because you ate your fill of the loaves' (6:26). He realises what is going on: 'You do not know him [God]' (7:28); 'You know neither me nor my Father' (8:19). He can ask directly: 'Why do you not understand what I say? It is because you cannot accept my word' (8:43).

Jesus is the one who knows the Father

'Very truly, I tell you, we speak of what we know and testify to what we have seen' (3:11). Jesus has knowledge of the Father that comes from being close to his heart. He is empathic: 'I know him, because I am from him, and he sent me' (7:29). He affirms: 'You do not know him. But I know him; if I were to say that I do not know him, I would be a liar like you. But I do know him and I keep his word' (8:55). He can say directly to God: 'Righteous Father, the world does not know you, but I know you; and these know that you have sent me' (17:25). 'My testimony is valid because I know where I have come from and where I am going, but you do not know where I come from or where I am going' (8:14; see also 13:3). One thing is certain: Jesus 'knows all things' (16:30).

Jesus shares this knowledge in relationship. That is what friends do. 'I do not call you servants any longer, because the servant does not know what the master is doing; but I have called you friends, because I have made known to you everything that I have heard from my Father' (15:15). As the prologue puts it: 'No one has ever seen God. It is God the only Son, who is close to the Father's heart, who has made him known' (1:18). Jesus lies on the Father's bosom and learns the deepest truths. He comes to share these. Principally, he is the revealer: 'The words that you gave to me I have given to them…

I have given them your word' (17:8, 14). He continues: 'I made your name known to them, and I will make it known, so that the love with which you have loved me may be in them, and I in them' (17:26).

Encountering the divine in John's gospel

For John, encounter–experience–discovery leads to knowledge. It springs from relationship: 'This is eternal life, that they may know you, the only true God, and Jesus Christ whom you have sent' (17:3). It is in encounter that discovery is made.

The Samaritan community are not content with hearing about Jesus second-hand from the witness of the woman at the well. They want first-hand experience and ask Jesus to stay with them a while. Then they can say to the woman: 'It is no longer because of what you said that we believe, for we have heard for ourselves, and we know that this is truly the Saviour of the world' (4:42) This is, indeed, 'saving knowledge'.

The man born blind is able to make a similar testimony: 'One thing I do know, that though I was blind, now I see' (9:25). He has literally received the touch of Jesus and had his eyes opened to glimpse the divine in Jesus.

Peter can make his confession only in the light of personal discovery. It is only after his encounter with the bread of life that he can say: 'We have come to believe and know that you are the Holy One of God' (6:69). First, he must see and eat.

The disciples experience shifts in perception when it comes to knowing the risen Christ. In the story by the Sea of Galilee in chapter 21, John tells us that knowledge comes through encounter and recognition: 'Just after daybreak, Jesus stood on the beach; but the disciples did not know that it was Jesus' (21:4). At a distance, physical and spiritual, the disciples cannot experience the risen one. It is only after they respond to his invitation, 'Come and have breakfast', that things change in the very process of approaching him: 'Now none of the disciples dared to ask him, "Who are you?" because they knew it was the Lord' (21:12). As they neared him in his physicality, they began to experience him and feel his risen presence, and the disciples came to *know* it was indeed the Lord. Thomas reaches his acclamation 'My Lord and my God!' only after encountering the risen Christ in his physicality (chapter 20).

For John, knowledge of the divine comes by engaging with the earthy, dusty Jesus, the Word who affirms and celebrates flesh by taking it on himself. Knowledge of the divine, for John, comes through encounter with the real, historical Jesus, not by fleeing into an abstract world of ideas. The corporeal world is not to be escaped but embraced. It is through the flesh and blood of Jesus that revelation comes, that theophany happens – not by some mystical ascent to the spiritual world. The physical world is to be approached with discernment and deep looking. Scholar James Gaffney in his study 'Believing and knowing in the fourth gospel' concludes:

> The distinctive meaning I should associate with knowing is that it is a kind of discernment of signs, a quality of insight into the transcendental reference of various symbolisms, ambiguities and veiled allusions… In knowing, one perceives that the signs, the works and so forth are pointing to something beyond their superficial selves.[9]

The fourth gospel's invitation to develop a sixth sense of 'knowing' is a call to penetrate beneath the surface of things, a refusal to stay on the surface, an utter openness to recognising and welcoming the shining out of the *Logos*. As Orthodox theologian Dumitru Stăniloae puts it: 'God sparkles then from everything.'[10]

· · · · · · · · · · · · · · · · · · ·

Spirituality of knowing

The mind in the heart

Echoing the Johannine tradition, the symbol of the heart has come to represent an awareness of the divine in a wide range of traditions. The writer of Ephesians had prayed: 'With the eyes of your heart enlightened, you may know what is the hope to which he has called you, what are the riches of his glorious inheritance among the saints' (1:18). Augustine experienced an inner listlessness: 'Our hearts are restless 'til they rest in you.' Benedict's *Rule* begins with the words, 'Listen carefully, my son and daughter, to the master's instructions and attend to them with the ear of your heart.'[11] Richard Baxter's hymn invites us: 'With a well-tuned heart sing thou the songs of love', while Charles Wesley pens the great hymn 'O for a heart to praise my God'.

This flows into Orthodox theology. As Ware explains:

> The heart signifies the deep self; it is the seat of wisdom and understanding, the place where our moral decisions are made, the inner shrine in which we experience divine grace and the indwelling of the Holy Trinity. It indicates the human person as a 'spiritual subject', created in God's image and likeness.[12]

Ware goes on: 'Here is no head–heart dichotomy, for the intellect is *within* the heart. The heart is the meeting point between body and soul, between the subconscious, conscious and supraconscious, between the human and the divine.'[13] Simeon the New Theologian writes of *moving* or relocating the mind to the heart:

> The mind should be in the heart... Keep your mind there (in the heart), trying by every possible means to find the place where the heart is, in order that, having found it, your mind should constantly abide there. Wrestling thus, your mind will find the place of the heart.[14]

What kind of knowledge can we seek? Writing in this Orthodox tradition, Maximos in the seventh century puts it:

> When the intellect (*nous*) practises contemplation, it advances in spiritual knowledge... The intellect is granted the grace of theology when, carried on wings of love... it is taken up into God and with the help of the Holy Spirit discerns – as far as this is possible for the human intellect – the qualities of God.[15]

Such knowledge is transforming: 'The intellect joined to God for long periods through prayer and love becomes wise, good, powerful, compassionate, merciful and long-suffering; in short, it includes with itself almost all the divine qualities.'[16]

In Orthodox spirituality, spiritual knowledge invites participation in God. As Gregory Palamas of Mount Athos (14th century), a main proponent of the prayer of *hesychia* (stillness), puts it: 'In prayer... man is called to *participation* in divine life: this participation is also the true knowledge of God.'[17] In his controversy with the Calabrian philosopher Barlaam, Palamas is insistent: 'But hesychasts know that the purified and illuminated mind, when clearly participating in the grace of God, also beholds other mystical and supernatural visions.'[18] Palamas and Maximos represent developments from the seminal thinking of Evagrius of Pontus (345–99) who very succinctly expressed the intermingling waters of spirituality and theology: 'He who prays is a theologian; a theologian is one who prays.'[19]

Indeed, such an approach heals the divide between mind and heart and opens a path to wholeness. Father Matthew of Mount Athos explains:

> True theology is coming to know God. It comes down to the difference between assimilating and accumulating. It is far more important to assimilate knowledge of God than accumulate ideas from books. The church needs theologians equipped with a spiritual life. It is the mind *and* the heart

working together: one integrated whole. The whole person needs to approach God using *all* the faculties of human being.[20]

Prayer and perception

A number of writers talk of prayer as a means of perception and as a way of knowing. Moltmann contrasts two approaches in epistemology. In modern scientific methods, he maintains, we know in order to achieve mastery, to gain possession of our subject. But there is a second way:

> Meditation is in fact an ancient method of arriving at knowledge which has not been pushed aside by our modern activism… Meditation is pre-eminently a way of sensory perception, of receiving, of absorbing and participating… The act of perception transforms the perceiver… Perception confers communion. We know in order to participate, not in order to dominate.[21]

For John Macquarrie, prayer helps to heal the human experience of fragmentedness and individualistic isolation, enabling the pray-er to see the world as a whole: 'Prayer enables us to see things in perspective… Prayer changes our vision of the world… Prayer interprets the world.'[22] Rowan Williams describes contemplative prayer as involving 'the project of reconditioning perception'.[23]

Watts and Williams in their study *The Psychology of Religious Knowing* are cautious about assigning a directly cognitive role to prayer, but they can see that significant shifts in perception take place in the practice of prayer:

> Indeed it is doubtful whether the 'acquisition of knowledge' is at all an appropriate way to describe the cognitive changes that take place in prayer. Prayer is probably better described as the *reinterpretation* of what is in some sense already known than as an exercise in the acquisition of knowledge.[24]

For Williams and Watts, prayer is 'an exercise in the interpretation of experience' and they find attribution theory helpful in understanding this process, in which religious people attribute events to God.[25] Prayer, especially the quiet, reflective type, becomes the place where real discernment is possible, where we see things with fresh eyes. Ann and Barry Ulanov in *Primary Speech* write of the transformations in perception that can take place in the course of prayer:

> This means we are living now in rearranged form. We are the same persons and yet radically different... The theme that dominates our lives now is the effort to correspond with grace. We want to go with the little signs and fragments of new being given us in prayer.[26]

Thus, prayer entails the risk of change, in which, little by little, perceptions are revised, self-acceptance grows and contradictions, if not resolved, become better understood. Effective prayer is, then, not about seeking to influence God, but about allowing God to do extraordinary things in us. But it requires of us the ability to silence our own admonitions and advice-giving to God, which can be a feature of intercessory prayer (as if we were advising the Almighty what he should do next). It requires us to come to a place of vulnerability and receptivity before God.

Prayer as discernment

John's gospel gives hints and clues about discernment when it describes Christ's prayerful communion with the Father in terms of glimpsing his will: 'The Son can do nothing on his own but only what he sees the Father doing... The Father loves the Son and shows him all that he himself is doing' (5:19–20). The Ignatian tradition celebrates the discovery of discernment in prayer, which develops this alertness.[27]

Hassel, writing out of the Ignatian tradition, identifies four levels of awareness in prayer.[28] The first level, the sensuous, embraces surface impressions gained through the five senses and swings of mood; he assigns vocal prayer and outward disciplines to this level. A second level, the physical-vital, enables us to access the power of pains or pleasures, fatigue or energy, which he links to active, reflective, meditative types of prayer. A third level, the psychological-psychic, goes deeper: 'The deep sorrows and the pure joys of this level totally permeate a person's being and consciousness.'[29] Here, Hassel locates more profound prayer experiences of fear, doubt, security or fulfilment and a kind of prayer that might unite the feelings with the imagination. At a fourth level, the 'prayer of simplicity' or 'simple being' sustains the pray-er throughout the upheavals of life, providing a continuity and stability beneath extremes of joy or sorrow, testifying to a sense of God's faithfulness. This, says Hassel, is the level at which one can discern the significance of what Ignatius called consolations and desolations. While these levels may be an oversimplification, they invite us to go ever deeper in our prayer and discernment.

The search for wisdom

John's gospel summons us to discover the *Logos* – the *Sophia*/ wisdom of God – throughout creation and in every human encounter. This quest for wisdom is a theme occupying modern writers.[30] David Ford calls attention in this information age to our sense of being overwhelmed by an excess of information and data. The challenge is to dare to swim in the river or ocean of wisdom:

> We have to swim in wisdom. If we try to stay in control through information, knowledge and skills, keeping our feet safely on the bottom of the ocean, we drown. So we see an educational system drowning in information, knowledge and skills and rarely even attending to the question: how can we learn and teach wisdom?[31]

As Louth points out, the danger is that if knowledge becomes viewed as an object of consumption, the one who knows becomes consumer rather than contemplator.[32] Writing from a scientific philosophical standpoint, Mary Midgley challenges all educators and students in the fundamental question of her book *Wisdom, Information and Wonder*. She argues that, since the rise of the professions, a body of knowledge has been valued as the goal to be sought, sometimes leading to narrow and isolated specialisms and the 'fear of facing the large questions'.[33] Knowledge is not for storage but for living: 'If thinking is our professional concern, the wisdom and wonder are our business: information-storage, though often useful, is just an accidental convenience.'[34]

For the Christian, the goal becomes not acquisition of information but inhabited wisdom. Hardy argues that wisdom is not an abstract, elusive, substance-like notion or hypostatisation that somehow lies behind all things. He points out that in both the Hebrew tradition and Pauline writings, wisdom is to be located and lived within the materiality and particularity of the demands of daily life in society, reordering our sense of reality by discerning God's presence and kingdom in the world. For the Christian, wisdom is incarnated and lived in the 'alienations of life'.[35]

Knowing and praying

Ford and Hardy in their book *Living in Praise* challenge us to invite the divine into our minds and hearts:

> We see knowing and praising God to be intrinsic to each other… Our conclusion about the rationality of knowing and praising God is that in this movement not only is God known… but also God enhances our rational powers. By knowing the reality of God we are changed by it, not only morally but also rationally. We are freed from the fixations and obsessions of reason… and are gently opened to being knit into a reality that is delightful as well as true. Then we realise that our very capacity to know and enjoy God has only been kept alive by the respect of God.[36]

If we define prayer as 'talking to God', we condemn ourselves to monologue. But if we start to think of the practice of prayer in terms of growing awareness of God, of discernment, of deep knowing, we open ourselves to fresh discovery of God and ourselves. John's gospel itself is a wisdom text, the fruit of deep prayer and theological reflection. It is testimony to a deeper kind of knowing, a honing of 'a sense of the divine'. As Simeon the New Theologian put it:

> He who gives us that which is above the senses, also endows us, through the grace of the Holy Spirit, with another sense which is above the senses, in order that we may clearly and purely apprehend his gifts and blessings, which are above the senses.[37]

. . . .

Questions for reflection

1 What questions do you have for God? Name them, articulate them.

2 How would you sum up the character of your own quest for God?

3 How are you advancing in spiritual knowledge? What helps, and what hinders?

4 What is your experience of perceptions shifting during the course of reflective prayer?

Prayer exercise

Take a walk in order to develop your sixth sense, your sensing of the divine. This can be in the beauty of creation or in a dreary housing estate or industrial landscape. Leave your comfort zone. Rule nothing out. Become present to your environment. Let physicality lead to spirituality, the concrete to prayer, the seen world to the unseen. Through your physical senses, come to sense the divine. Shift perceptions. Come to knowledge of God!

Practise the art of theological reflection. Ask yourself: where am I glimpsing God or feeling his presence? What things speak to me of the divine? Maybe read your environs symbolically and look for elements that somehow represent the sort of God you believe in.

Open up your awareness and consciousness of the divine, experience a deep knowing. Conclude with thanksgiving. Celebrate your potential and your capacity: made to discover God, all your faculties attuned to this. Realise what you are capable of!

3

Relocating: a sense of place

From the outset, John's gospel reveals an acute sense of place. The disciples of the Baptist ask Jesus: 'Where are you staying?' and he responds invitingly: 'Come and see' (1:38–39). This summons resounds across the gospel. We are invited to share in a journey of discovery. We are invited in the fourth gospel to accompany Jesus as he traverses the land as a pilgrim and traveller. We will get a sense that the author of the fourth gospel has a first-hand knowledge of the land, its valleys and its plains. Bruce Schein observes:

> John has probably been the most neglected gospel in terms of the touchable and seeable background of the first century... John constantly keeps the reader informed with precise geographical data... To enter into this 'feeling' with and for the land with eyes, ears, hands, and hearts is important for a complete understanding of the Johannine setting.[1]

In this chapter, we will begin to get a sense of location, setting and environment. After noting places in the fourth gospel not occurring in the other gospels, we focus on the dramatic significance of four locations unique to John: we will enter the forbidden territory of Samaria and discover the forgotten threshold of the Pool of Siloam; we will ascend the end-time mountain of the Mount of Olives and discover the gardens of tryst and trust.

Discovering the land

In the fourth gospel, we travel to several locations in Galilee and Judea that are unique to John, places not found in the other gospels. John takes us twice to Cana in Galilee (2:1–11; 4:46–54). We discover Jacob's Well at the village of Sychar (4:3–6). We find John baptising at Aenon near Salim, where 'water was abundant' (3:23). John alone mentions the name Tiberias (6:1, 23; 21:1) referring to the alternative name of the Sea of Galilee, taken from the Roman city on the western shore and named after the Caesar. John leads us into the wilderness at Ephraim (11:54) and he takes us to the far, eastern shore of the river, to Bethany beyond the Jordan (1:28).

Noticing the details

John has a sharp eye, a fascination for the details at such sites and keen attentiveness to physicality and environment. He tells us that Jacob's Well is deep, and it is in a field (4:5, 11). There is a lot of water at Aenon near Salim (3:23). Grass covers hills above Sea of Galilee (6:10). Bethany is two miles from Jerusalem (11:18). Lazarus' tomb is a cave (11:38). The tomb of Jesus has a low entrance ('he bent down to look in', 20:5). We learn details about the Jerusalem temple: forecourts accommodate a range of animals (2:13–16); the porticoes of Solomon offer shelter in winter (10:22–23); the treasury is a suitable place for teaching (8:20). John takes us to visit the Bethesda, describing a pool near the Sheep Gate with five colonnades or porticoes (a line of columns supporting a roof-like structure, 5:2). He tells us that the house of the High Priest has a courtyard, with a fire in it (18:15, 18). John records that Jesus was crucified at Golgotha, the place of the skull, which was located 'near the city', meaning just outside the city walls (19:17). Uniquely, he tells us that there is a garden close by, in which an unused tomb had been carved into the rock (19:41–42). We even learn that there is an inviting beach on the shore of Lake Galilee (21:4)!

The countryside

'After this Jesus and his disciples went into the Judean countryside' (3:22). John takes us on an itinerary across the land, with its physical landscape celebrated at many points, giving allusions that trigger the imagination in the reader. We can picture Jesus:

Encountering the wilderness
Not only does Jesus enter the desert when seeking baptism, but he also makes two further retreats in the desert: once after his confrontation with Jewish scribes (10:40) and, significantly, a second foray prior to the Passion (11:54). Unique to the fourth gospel, these give us glimpses into Jesus' own need for silence and solitude. We also note that John's narrative, like Mark's, begins in the Judean desert: 'The Jews sent priests and Levites from Jerusalem to ask [John], "Who are you?"' (1:19): his inquisitors journey from the city to the desert. The Baptist describes himself as 'a voice of one crying out in the wilderness' (1:23).

Wading across the river
There is no other way except fording the river to reach Bethany beyond Jordan, located on the far eastern bank of the river, which Jesus visits at least twice (1:28; 3:26; 10:40). He also fords the Kidron brook (18:1).

Climbing mountains
Jesus ascends the hills above the Sea of Galilee for the sign about the bread of life (6:3, 15). Reference is made to Mount Gerazim (4:20) in his discussion with the woman at Jacob's Well. Jesus retreats to the Mount of Olives (8:1).

Traversing the stormy lake
Jesus crosses 'to the other side of the Sea of Galilee' (6:1). Later, he walks on the surface of the turbulent waves (6:19).

Entering hostile no-go areas

In chapter 4, as we shall see, Jesus crosses the boundary into the territory of Samaria, not recommended for a Jewish person.

The city

John knows the city of Jerusalem very well. He mentions a number of locations that do not feature in the other gospels. He describes the five arches of the Pool of Bethesda and its location near the Sheep Gate (5:2). He gives special significance, as we shall see, to the Pool of Siloam (9:1–9). The first is north of the temple, the other south, and both function in relation to the temple.

In the account of the Passion, John is keen to give details of specific locations. The praetorium (18:28, 33; 19:9) is the headquarters of the Roman military governor and probably to be identified with the Antonia Fortress looming over the temple area. The stone pavement (Greek: *lithostrotos*), also known as *Gabbatha* ('raised place' in Aramaic) was located outside the praetorium, and was the place where Pilate made his judgements (19:13).

John gives special mention to Bethany near Jerusalem as a place of retreat in the company of dear friends, as we shall see. Let's travel now with Jesus the pilgrim and explore a little more four particularly significant sites.

1 Entering forbidden territory: penetrating Samaria's border

In order to make a journey from Jerusalem to Galilee, Jesus had the choice of three routes. There was the Via Maris, the magnificent Roman road that followed the coastal plain, the main trade route indeed from Egypt to Mesopotamia. This was an undemanding road, favoured by traders and merchants. A second route followed the Jordan Valley. There, one could walk in the great rift valley within sight of the river itself. A third route was tricky and unpopular, for it passed through the Samaritan territory. It was difficult in places, because these are the central highlands of the country, with steeply sided hills and meandering ravines. Indeed, a valley south of Shechem is called, to this day, the Valley of the Thieves, because historically it was a place of ambush and attack. But, of course, this third route was undesirable from a Jewish point of view, because, as John reminds us, 'Jews have no dealings with the Samaritans' (4:9, KJV). In Jewish eyes, Samaritans were hated pariahs, half-castes, religiously impure, and to take this route would defile and contaminate the Jewish traveller. They were a despised underclass, a bastard people. Ever since the Assyrian deportation of the population in 722BC and the subsequent repopulating of the area with people of different bloods, Jews had looked upon Samaritans with disdain. Samaria had become a hostile, no-go area.

However, John tells us: '[Jesus] left Judea and started back to Galilee. But he *had* to go through Samaria' (4:3–4, emphasis mine). Why did he *have* to take this route? What divine imperative impelled Jesus to choose this most treacherous way? It is vital for Jesus to take this route; it is necessary for one reason alone: Jesus wanted the disciples to have the experience of travelling through liminal terrain where they would be profoundly changed. Jesus was insistent on this passage to Galilee because he wanted his disciples to enter marginal, despised territory where many of their most cherished ideas about God and humanity would be shattered and reconstructed. For Jesus, there was simply no other way!

In John's perspective, Jesus takes his disciples to Samaria for no less a reason than to expose them to radical paradigm shifts, to lead them to a breakthrough in attitudes. As we read chapter 4, we see all kinds of shifts in perception taking place – in the woman at the well, in the local villagers and also in the disciples. Jesus wants to help them transcend traditional categories of thought. He wants to liberate them from the straitjackets and prisons of inherited prejudice and stereotyping.

2 The forgotten threshold

For many years it has puzzled biblical interpreters and preachers. Why did Jesus send the blind man, of John 9, to the Pool of Siloam? This has been a conundrum on several levels. First, Jesus does not heal the blind in this way in other accounts. To be sure, there are several stories about the cure of closed eyes – we think, for example, of blind Bartimaeus (Mark 10:46–52). Jesus even uses spittle on one other occasion (Mark 8:22–26). But here, after anointing his eyes with clay from the earth, he commands the blind man to go down to the Pool of Siloam and wash. What would be the significance of that? Second, archaeologists have long been confused over the function of the narrow pool they saw named Siloam. Was it something to do with the city's water supply, given its proximity to the ancient water source for Jerusalem, the Gihon Spring? Hezekiah had brought this water supply within the city during the Assyrian threat and it is still possible to walk through the 225 feet of the tunnel that now supplies Siloam. Was its purpose, then, to provide access to this supply so it could be used for domestic purposes?

Since 2004, stunning archaeological discoveries have been made at the pool, which reveal its true extent and its real function: it is a *limen*, a threshold, for pilgrims entering upon Jerusalem after their dirty and exhausting trek through the desert. We shall take a fresh look at this story, and, for the first time, explore its astonishing role in the spirituality of the episode.

The site in question is the lowest point of the ancient city of David, which was first developed on the southern spur of the Ophel Ridge around 1000BC. While the temple came to be built at the top of the ridge – the high place – this site developed at the foot of the hill, on its southern edge. Visitors to what has been called in the past 'the Pool of Siloam' have been shown a narrow, oblong-shaped pond of Byzantine age. In the fifth century, Empress Eudokia built a basilica over this pool to celebrate the miracle of John 9. The basilica has long disappeared – destroyed by the Persians in 614 – and all that can be seen is an unimpressive pool measuring just ten feet across, with a few stumps of the basilica's pillars remaining.

In the summer of 2004, Israeli archaeologist Eli Shukron began to take another look at the ground just south of this site, because work needed to be done to improve Jerusalem's drainage system. He discovered some huge stone ledges cut into the rock. Archaeologists continued to dig and identified several flights of steps leading to a vast, open pool. These had been covered over with mud and debris sliding down the hill since the end of the first century. This site was probably abandoned after AD70 when Titus destroyed the temple.[2]

As excavations continued, the scope of the discovery became clearer. This was the real Pool of Siloam – the narrow Byzantine pond, long venerated by pilgrims, was just a feeder bath for it! Each side measures a staggering 225 feet: the pool is bigger than the size of an Olympic swimming pool, accommodating a substantial and impressive body of water. Indeed, there was nothing to compare with it within the city of Jerusalem: it was a breathtaking oasis. Three flights of five broad, monumental steps, each flight separated by a wide landing, lead down into the pool. In fact, only half of the pool has yet been excavated, but enough to reveal that the Pool of Siloam was a spacious and inspiring tract of water on the very edge of the ancient city of David. So what was its function?

It was more than just a reservoir for a thirsty city: it was a *mikveh* – a ritual bath or immersion pool for pilgrims arriving in the holy city. It is right next to the gate in the city walls of Jesus' time, and marks the entry point for travellers arriving via the Hinnom Valley from the west and via the Kidron Valley from the east and from the Judean desert. It is literally the threshold of the city and pilgrims would cleanse themselves here before making the ascent of a steep staircase up to the temple mount. This staircase has also recently been revealed by archaeologists and, since 2012, it has become possible to retrace the steps of arriving pilgrims and ascend the slope of the original Mount Zion towards the area of the second temple. The Pool of Siloam, then, functions only in relation to the temple itself: it is the ablution pool for sweaty and dirty pilgrims! At the foot of Mount Zion, it is a welcoming place for worshippers.

What are the implications of this discovery for our reading of John 9? What is the meaning of Jesus' words to the man: 'Go and wash in the Pool of Siloam?' And, so what? What does it mean to us today? It turns out to be a double imperative from the lips of Jesus.

Washing in the waters of pilgrimage

The first transition or movement for the blind man is both physical and spiritual and touches on his very identity. Jesus wants the man to position himself at the point of the threshold. He will receive his healing only at this particular place – not even at the place where Jesus first met him. He needs to apply the water to his muddy, stinging eyes. What will be the first thing that this man sees in his entire life – given that he has been blind from birth? His opening eyes will first see a flight of stone steps beckoning him up the hill to the very temple of God. He will see an inviting staircase, leading, it seems, to heaven. And he will know this: he is accepted. He is wanted. He is a child of God! All his life he has been exiled from the temple precincts because of his disability. The sick and imperfect were not allowed to get anywhere close to the Holy of Holies. All his life, he has been excluded from the holiest place by traditional regulations. But now he sees God's invitation – he sees, as it were, God's hand beckoning him up those steps. This was Jesus' longing, that God's house should be a place for all people.

What a healing needed to take place in those waters of Siloam! Not only the restoration of the man's eyes but the deep healing of his spirit. All his life he had been an outcast, rejected, not good enough – even a threat to the purity of others. He had been stigmatised and ostracised. People would gossip and speculate about him, just like the disciples when they asked: 'Rabbi, who sinned, this man or his parents, that he was born blind?' To compound his suffering, the man had to live with guilt: 'What have I done to deserve this?' Jesus was emphatic: 'Neither this man, nor his parents sinned; he was born blind that God's works might be revealed in him' (9:2–3). In John's perspective, this episode is not a miracle but a *sign*: an indicator of the type of kingdom Jesus came to inaugurate.

Moreover, it is Jesus' wish that the man locate himself precisely at the place where pilgrims arrive from their dusty and exhausting journeys. He is to discover for himself the joy and exhilaration of becoming a pilgrim to the holy place. Now he takes his rightful place among the pilgrim people of God. He finds himself walking in the footsteps of Abraham and David. He finds himself now on a spiritual quest and a spiritual journey. Ascending the flight of steps towards the crest of the holy hill, towards the temple sanctuary, he discovers himself to be a pilgrim and can for the first time celebrate the psalm of ascent: 'I was glad when they said to me, "Let us go to the house of the Lord!" Our feet are standing within your gates, O Jerusalem!' (Psalm 122:1–2). He is empowered by Christ. Where formerly he had been a passive recipient of alms, now he can take responsibility for himself, as he steps confidently towards the temple sanctuary. And, like the man born blind wading through the waters of Siloam, we too are invited to plunge ourselves into the waters of God's life-changing grace.[3]

Wading in the waters of the Spirit

For Jesus, the waters of the Pool of Siloam speak powerfully of the Holy Spirit, for it is in the context of the great Jewish ceremony of *Simchat Beit Hashoeva*, meaning 'the Rejoicing of the water-drawing', the great day of the Feast of Tabernacles, that he makes a glorious promise concerning the Spirit of God:

> On the last day of the festival, the great day, while Jesus was standing there, he cried out, 'Let anyone who is thirsty come to me, and let the one who believes in me drink. As the scripture has said, "Out of the believer's heart shall flow rivers of living

water."' Now he said this about the Spirit, which believers in him were to receive; for as yet there was no Spirit, because Jesus was not yet glorified.

JOHN 7:37–39

Jesus was joining in the temple liturgy where Ezekiel's vision (chapter 47) was proclaimed to the pilgrims: a spring of God's generous blessing bursts forth from under the altar of the temple, spilling out to bring renewal to the whole world. The water gets deeper and deeper as Ezekiel follows the line of the river from the holy city out into the deserts. At first, the prophet can wade in the water, but soon it comes up right to his waist, so he must swim in the river of God's blessing. The tabernacles festival reached a climax when, on the last day, a solemn ceremony celebrating this vision carried up to the temple in a golden vessel waters from the Pool of Siloam. It was a joyous, colourful and noisy procession accompanied by musicians with harp, drum, cymbal and the *shofar* trumpets. The water was poured out as a sign of God's blessing in 'the age to come' – since they originate with the Gihon Spring, and one of the rivers of paradise is called the Gihon (Genesis 2:13), the waters came to symbolise the hope of a paradise restored: that the waters of Eden will one day flow again. Jesus was watching this ritual when he cried out his urgent, awesome promise. You do not have to wait until the last day! With his glorification on the cross, the Spirit will be unleashed as an overflowing stream to renew all of creation.[4]

When, in the context of the temple (7:14) and referring to the waters of Siloam, Jesus echoes Ezekiel's prophecy and makes his glorious promise, what does he mean? How can the Spirit come to us as a stream of living water and flow in us and out through us? Jesus alludes to the energy of the Spirit. He is talking of the cascade of the Spirit, the movement of the Spirit, the empowering of the Spirit, his energy within us. He speaks of an inflow and an overflow. The Spirit comes to us and then, bubbling up like a mountain brook, streams out to others. Jesus is talking about the renewing and refreshing grace of the Spirit. As sparkling, living water invigorates and enlivens weary bodies, so the Spirit makes us new, replenishing and restoring parched souls: this is the healing grace of the Spirit, echoing Ezekiel's vision of trees with leaves for healing thriving alongside the riverbank (Ezekiel 47:12).

According to John's chronology, Christ's promise relating to the waters of Siloam was a recent event, taking place not long before he met the man born blind, so his command 'Go, wash in Siloam' clearly evokes the gift of the Spirit, bubbling up as Siloam's waters themselves emerge from deep within the earth near Gihon's mighty spring. In saying 'Go, wash in Siloam', Jesus is saying: 'Go, and feel the fresh waters on your skin. Go and drink deep of the Spirit! Open your eyes and see the river of God!' Indeed, part of the water-drawing ceremony at Siloam included the words: 'We belong to God and our eyes are turned to God!'[5] In this transition, the man born blind moves from spiritual aridity and thirst to the joy of imbibing the divine Spirit.

Ultimately, this episode makes sense only in relation to its spatial setting: the threshold, the pilgrim's ablution pool, the nearby desert. John is asking us to open our eyes wide in order to notice how healing grace is encountered in the physicality of the earth.

3 The mountain

In the days before his Passion, Jesus leads his disciples to an extraordinary liminal place, the Mount of Olives. It is the bridge between the desert and the city, the link between time and eternity, and the intersection between heaven and earth.

First, it is the threshold between the city and the desert, for it marks the ending of the desert and the brink of the city, rising to a height of 2,500 feet above sea level. Bethany, the village of Martha, Mary and Lazarus, lies on the eastern flank of the mountain, facing the desert. The western slope of the mountain, just over the crest from Bethany, faces the holy city itself. The Mount of Olives has been called the numinous threshold of the city, for all pilgrims, as they make their journey up from the deep rift valley to the city, must pause at the Mount of Olives, to catch their breath and to see the amazing panorama of the glistening city below. It is literally and symbolically a watershed: not only does the climate change on this mountain range (desert to the east, Mediterranean-type to the west), but also one's very heart and mind change as one climbs the mountain in preparation for the encounter with the holy city.

Second, it is the threshold between time and eternity. It is the eschatological mountain, becoming the focus for hopes for God's advent at the end of time. Zechariah predicts: 'On that day his feet shall stand on the Mount of Olives, which lies before Jerusalem on the east; and the Mount of Olives shall be split in two from east to west by a very wide valley' (Zechariah 14:4). This is the cataclysmic vision of Zechariah in the sixth century before Christ. In a gentler image, he had written: 'Rejoice greatly, O daughter of Zion! Shout aloud, O daughter of Jerusalem! Lo, your king comes to you; triumphant and victorious is he, humble and riding on a donkey, on a colt, the foal of a donkey' (Zechariah 9:9). In his apocalyptic dream, Joel sees God gathering the nations for judgement in the valley below (Joel 3:2). So the Mount of Olives becomes a place of judgement and hope, but all these dreams look to the far future for their fulfilment. These are visions of the end of times and, here, Jesus gives his apocalyptic discourse (Mark 13). To this day, the Mount of Olives is covered with hundreds of tombs: a vast Jewish cemetery clings to its western side, while Christian graves lie in the valley and Muslim tombs stand by the city walls. All three traditions await the coming of God and the dawn of the judgement day at this location. Humanity's longings for a new world are focused here.[6]

This is a mountain that pilgrims must cross in order to reach the holy city. There is no other way, from the east. In Hebrew, the word for pilgrimage is *aliyah*, meaning 'to go up'. With pilgrims of old, we climb towards Jerusalem. With them, we make our own the psalms of ascent (Psalms 120—134): 'I lift up my eyes to the hills – from where will my help come?' (Psalm 121:1); 'As the mountains surround Jerusalem, so the Lord surrounds his people' (Psalm 125:2).

The astonishing story of John 11 can be understood only by an appreciation of the theological symbolism of the Mount of Olives.[7] According to John's chronology and geographical perspective, before his final journey to Jerusalem, Jesus positions himself deep in the desert, at the very point of the exodus and of his baptism. John says: 'He went away again across the Jordan to the place where John had been baptising earlier, and he remained there' (10:40). Jesus waits at the very point of the ancient salvation, for it is here at the great river that Joshua had led the Hebrews into the promised land at the end of their wearisome journey of 40 years (Joshua 3). Jesus is going back to where it all began, as if to suggest that he might be leading a new exodus journey into freedom. It is also precisely the place where he had received that amazing affirmation at his baptism: 'You are my beloved Son.' It is the place where he had seen the heavens torn apart, opening up in his ministry a new way to God. Now Jesus goes back there and 'he remains there'. He waits. He prepares himself for his last journey to Jerusalem. In John's perspective, what occasions his final ascent to the city is the call of Martha and Mary. John makes a very close connection between the raising of Lazarus and the events of the Passion (see 11:45–53; 12:9–11) and, of course, it is the starting point for Jesus' descent into the city in his Palm Sunday procession. In the account of John 11, Jesus leads his people into a revolutionary new view of God on this mountain, requiring major shifts or transitions in their understanding.[8]

From God of the end to God of the now

When Jesus promises that Lazarus will rise again, Martha confesses her faith in the general resurrection at the end of times: 'I know that he will rise again in the resurrection on the last day' (11:24). She has hope in a distant future event – part of traditional Jewish faith. This tenet is of course the usual and accepted doctrine that the Mount of

Olives will witness the final judgement and the resurrection of the dead – on doomsday – a belief, we have seen, that comes from the prophets Zechariah and Joel. Only on the far horizon of history will God act decisively and make all things new.

With Jesus, the future is now. He summons Martha to revolutionise her hope: 'I am the resurrection and the life. Those who believe in me, even though they die, will live' (11:25).[9] Jesus invites her to release her grip on dogmatic definitions and turns upside down the conservative traditional faith Martha expressed. He blows apart her inherited religious and respectable mindset. He smashes into pieces the remoteness of her hope by declaring that the eschatological, end-time 'life of the world to come' is already, right now, breaking into people's lives. He dares her to step out of her cocoon of inherited faith and make the leap of faith into this new revelation, asking: 'Do you believe this?' (11:26). Jesus, the resurrection and the life, stands on the very mountain that, with all its tombs, longs for the day of renewal. Martha is summoned to take the risk of trusting Jesus as the one who, even now, ushers in the new age.

4 The garden

When John locates Jesus and his actions in a garden, the reader immediately recognises the resonances and their significance. Two in particular stand out.

First, and most obviously, a reference to a garden evokes Genesis' primordial garden of Eden. This garden illustrates the goodness and givenness of creation, with its streams and trees: 'The earth brought forth vegetation: plants yielding seed of every kind, and trees of every kind bearing fruit with the seed in it. And God saw that it was good' (Genesis 1:12).[10] This garden is the place of creation where God forms man from the dust of the ground and breathes into him the breath of life (Genesis 2:7). This garden is a place of communion where once Adam and his creator walked together in the cool of the day (Genesis 3:8). But this garden is also a place of betrayal, deceit and disruption of the divine–human relationship.

The second garden evoked in the fourth gospel is the luxuriant, life-giving garden of the Song of Songs. At the centre of the Bible, this rich poem invites us to explore two themes in connection with the garden. First, it invites us to enjoy a spontaneous delight in the beauty of creation and to rediscover a sacramental approach to the world. In this wisdom literature, the garden becomes a meeting place for lovers, the place of the tryst, the bride and groom celebrating their love. But the Song of Songs also invites us to a second, darker theme in connection with the garden: the garden emerges not only as the place of personal communion, but also as the place of intense struggle. In heartbreak, the bridegroom finds 'a garden locked is my sister, my bride' (4:12). When the bride awakes from slumber, she finds that her lover has gone: 'I sought him, but did not find him; I called him, but he gave no answer' (5:6). The garden becomes a place of separation, of communion disrupted, of love unrequited. It becomes a place of unanswered questions: 'What is your beloved?' (5:9); 'Which way has your beloved turned?' (6:1). The poem ends with the bride's agonised cry: 'O you who dwell in the gardens, my companions are listening for your voice; let me hear it. Make haste, my beloved' (8:13–14). This double theme, of presence and absence, of communion and struggle, alerts us, like Eden, to the ambiguity and paradox of the symbol of the garden, a theme that is developed in the fourth gospel.

Garden of passion

> After Jesus had spoken these words, he went out with his disciples across the Kidron valley to a place where there was a garden, which he and his disciples entered. Now Judas, who betrayed him, also knew the place, because Jesus often met there with his disciples.
> JOHN 18:1–2

Jesus crosses a stream to enter Gethsemane. Here, the question Jesus repeats resounds across the centuries: 'Whom are you looking for?' Jesus in this garden twice declares: 'I am he,' evoking the 'I am' of the burning bush and the great 'I am' sayings of the fourth gospel, including the extraordinary words, 'Before Abraham was, I am' (8:58). Jesus enters this garden a free man, but soon he is bound and shackled by soldiers (18:12). Soon, the garden of peaceful friendship, much beloved by Jesus as a 'desert in the city', a favourite place of retreat, as John tells us (18:2), becomes a garden of violence. Not only do soldiers bear arms and weapons (18:3), but Peter also gets a knife out and stabs at the high priest's servant. Soon he will be challenged about this action: 'One of the slaves of the high priest, a relative of the man whose ear Peter had cut off, asked, "Did I not see you in the garden with him?"' (18:26). 'Did I not see you in the garden?' The words might have been said to Adam!

Garden of resurrection

If John is attentive to the setting of betrayal, he will soon celebrate the garden as the very place of salvation:

> The place where Jesus was crucified was near the city... Now there was a garden in the place where he was crucified, and in the garden there was a new tomb in which no one had ever been laid. And so, because it was the Jewish day of Preparation, and the tomb was nearby, they laid Jesus there.
> JOHN 19:20, 41–42

John is giving us two vital facts in his narrative. First, Jesus swings from a tree in the garden. If Eden had a tree of life at its centre, this garden is dominated by a life-giving and redemptive tree. If Eden had a tree of the knowledge of good and evil, which caused distress and disruption, John's garden has a tree of glory. A new creation is dawning, and paradise is being regained!

Second, John alone locates the tomb and the resurrection in a garden. The story of Mary Magdalene's encounter with the risen Lord has strong echoes of the Song of Songs, which refers to the garden (*kepos* in Greek) nine times: indeed Mary herself 'supposes him to be the gardener' (20:15).

Three striking features stand out:

The search

Mary Magdalene's dilemma is her search in the darkness for the body of Jesus:

> Early on the first day of the week, while it was still dark, Mary Magdalene came to the tomb and saw that the stone had been removed from the tomb. So she ran and went to Simon Peter and the other disciple, the one whom Jesus loved, and said to them, 'They have taken the Lord out of the tomb, and we do not know where they have laid him.'
>
> JOHN 20:1–2

This evokes the nocturnal quest of a woman seeking her lover in the Song of Songs:

> Upon my bed at night
>   I sought him whom my soul loves;
> I sought him, but found him not;
>   I called him, but he gave no answer.
> 'I will rise now and go about the city,
>   in the streets and in the squares;
> I will seek him whom my soul loves.'
>   I sought him, but found him not.
> The sentinels found me,
>   as they went about in the city.
> 'Have you seen him whom my soul loves?'
>
> SONG OF SONGS 3:1–3

At last, there is the hope of encounter, sensuously anticipated:

> I slept, but my heart was awake.
> Listen! my beloved is knocking.
> 'Open to me, my sister, my love,
>   my dove, my perfect one;
> for my head is wet with dew,
>   my locks with the drops of the night.'
> I had put off my garment;
>   how could I put it on again?
> I had bathed my feet;
>   how could I soil them?
> My beloved thrust his hand into the opening,
>   and my inmost being yearned for him.
> I arose to open to my beloved,
>   and my hands dripped with myrrh,
> my fingers with liquid myrrh,
>   upon the handles of the bolt.
> SONG OF SONGS 5:2–5

However, the lover is elusive:

> I opened to my beloved,
>   but my beloved had turned and was gone.
> My soul failed me when he spoke.
> I sought him, but did not find him;
>   I called him, but he gave no answer.
> SONG OF SONGS 5:6

In the garden of the fourth gospel, Mary asks the stranger: 'Sir, if you have carried him away, tell me where you have laid him, and I will take him away' (20:15). He replies: 'Do not hold on to me… I am ascending' (20:17). David Carr observes:

> This depiction of longing, like the Song of Songs, is a tease. It describes a Jesus who is longed for and present, yet also

unreachable… The text focuses on intense longing, though not specifically sexual desire. Her [Mary's] passionate longing is her greatest strength on this story. In it, she models the love that the Johannine Jesus calls on all his disciples to exhibit (John 13:34; 15:12, 17).[11]

The voice
The lover in the Song of Songs often refers to the voice of her beloved:

The voice of my beloved!
   Look, he comes,
leaping upon the mountains,
   bounding over the hills…
Let me see your face,
   let me hear your voice;
for your voice is sweet,
   and your face is lovely.
SONG OF SONGS 2:8, 14

But when she finally hears his voice, she is overwhelmed: 'My soul failed me when he spoke' (5:6).

In John's story, Mary Magdalene hears the question of the risen Christ: 'Woman, why are you weeping?' But it is only at that sublime moment when Jesus calls her by name that she can respond, 'Rabbouni! My teacher!' (20:16).

The turning
In his narrative, John strangely refers twice to a movement that has strong allusions with the Song of Songs. Two times John tells us that Mary makes a movement with her body: 'She turned round and saw Jesus standing there, but she did not know that it was Jesus' (20:14); 'Jesus said to her, "Mary!" She turned and said to him in Hebrew, "Rabbouni!"' (20:16). The Song makes a number of references to 'turning' – the women of Jerusalem cry out to the lover: 'Turn! Turn!' (6:13). This movement by Mary may be a metaphor of the 'turning'

of conversion; it may also be a further allusion to the sensuous language of the Song.[12] We shall explore further links in chapter 9.

We have seen in this chapter how attentive John is to the details of place. While celebrating this alertness to the local and the particular, it is important to recall that all is set within a cosmic perspective: literally so, for when John speaks of the world he uses the word *cosmos*. For John, there is a paradox in this widest of settings. The world is the object of God's love: 'For God so loved the world that he gave his only Son' (3:16). Yet it will reject him and his disciples: 'If the world hates you, be aware that it hated me before it hated you. If you belonged to the world, the world would love you as its own. Because you do not belong to the world, but I have chosen you out of the world – therefore the world hates you' (15:18–19). He goes on: 'In the world you face persecution. But take courage; I have conquered the world!' (16:33). John's prologue alerts us to this: 'The true light, which enlightens everyone, was coming into the world. He was in the world, and the world came into being through him; yet the world did not know him' (1:9–10). Moving between intimacy and ultimacy, John invites us to appreciate the small details of place without losing a sense of the bigger picture – of cosmic dimensions. In the fourth gospel, Jesus is at once the dusty pilgrim and traveller traversing the land, and the very creator Word made flesh!

· · · · · · · · · · · · · · · · · ·

Spirituality of place

The Benedictine tradition

The triple vows of the Benedictine *Rule* suggest a framework in which to understand and make sense of the sometimes conflicting dynamics of Christian discipleship today. We find ourselves caught between the pull of duty to others and the pull of developing the self, and the first two vows suggest a dialectic within which this tension can be not so much resolved as held creatively.

Benedict's vow of stability commits the monk to stay with a particular community for life. It is the first of the vows, because it is about the total surrender of one's life to God, within the particular setting and context of a group of people. In a world where people are rushing around in ever greater degrees of mobility, this commitment invites us to reconsider a rootedness in the here and now, an attentiveness to the needs of a particular community, and firmly rejects the temptation that 'the grass is greener elsewhere'.

The vow of *stabilitas* reminds us of the essentially incarnational nature of discipleship, and of the call to be fully present to a particular historical context. But this vow also calls us to consistency, to steadfastness, as Benedict puts it: 'to persevere in his stability' (58:9). It calls us to the rock of faithfulness and constancy in a sea of change and tempest of transition. In today's context, this vow is about not giving up, not giving way under the pressures that confront today's Christian, which include marginalisation and loss of respect in society. It is about rediscovering God's *hesed* or steadfast love and faithfulness, expressed in Paul's affirmation: 'I am confident of this, that the one who began a good work among you will bring it to completion' (Philippians 1:6).

Yet the biblical metaphors of 'standing in the evil day' (Ephesians 6:13) or 'remaining in the vine' (John 15:4) need also to be in conversation with the dynamic language of movement and motion with which Benedict both begins and ends his *Rule*:

- Run while you have the light of life (Prologue 13)
- Run on the path of God's commandments (Prologue 49)
- Hasten towards your heavenly home (73:8)

And so the vow of *stabilitas* stands in tension with Benedict's second vow of *conversatio morum*, the conversion of life, which calls for constant growth and change. This is an echo of the New Testament call to *metanoia*, turning again to God, and resonates with Paul's resolve: 'Straining forward to what lies ahead' (Philippians 3:13).

Such a commitment can be both liberating and unnerving. It invites us to let go of cherished and familiar ways of working, to be ready for risk-taking, open to experimental and provisional patterns of witness and ministry, which emerge as Christendom dissolves and the church discovers different ways of being in a post-Christian, post-modern world.[13] It calls us to accept the need for lifelong learning and continuous development. It requires of us both a thirst for fresh understanding of God's word and world, and also a vulnerability, a lowering of self-protective barriers, to be open to the God of surprises.

The Celtic tradition

The Celtic tradition celebrates the wonder and potential of the 'thin place', where the veil that separates heaven and earth is lifted, and where the door between two worlds seems to be poignantly ajar. This is often in wild places in the landscape. Philip Sheldrake tells us: 'Living on physical boundaries also symbolised a state of liminality – of living literally and spiritually on the margins or between two worlds, the material one and the spiritual one.'[14] Celtic Christians could experience sites in the natural world as thresholds of the divine. With Jacob, they could say of the landscape: 'How awesome is this place… This is the gate of heaven' (Genesis 28:17). John's gospel evokes this passage when Jesus says to Nathaniel: 'Very truly, I tell you, you will see heaven opened and the angels of God ascending and descending upon the Son of Man' (1:51). The Celtic psalter, traditionally ascribed to Oengus the Culdee, an Irish hermit of the ninth century, exults:

> My dear King, my own King, without pride, without sin, You created the whole world, eternal, victorious King.

King above the elements, King above the sun, King beneath the ocean, King of the north and south, the east and west, against you no enemy can prevail.

King of the mysteries, you existed before the elements, before the sun was set in the sky, before the waters covered the ocean floor; beautiful King, you are without beginning and without end.

King, you created the daylight and made the darkness; you are not arrogant or boastful, and yet strong and firm.

King you created the land out of shapeless mass, you carved the mountains and chiselled the valleys, and covered the earth with trees and grass.

King, you stretched out the sky above the earth, a perfect sphere like a perfect apple, and you decorated the sky with stars to shine at night.

King, you pierced the earth with springs from which pure water flows, to form streams and rivers across the land…

King, you measured each object and each span within the universe: the heights of the mountains and the depths of the oceans; the distance from the sun to the moon, and from star to star…

And you created men and women to be your stewards of the earth, always praising you for your boundless love.[15]

In the Celtic tradition, we see the paradox resurfacing: while we are alert to the particular manifestations of the divine in our own locale, we can rejoice in the wonder of the universe.

· · · · · · · · · · · · · · · · · · ·

Questions for reflection

1   In what particular places have you been surprised by God, even experiencing unexpected epiphany?

2   'The grass is greener on the other side.' How do you experience the paradox in Benedict's *Rule* between being utterly committed to a place (*stabilitas*) and yet being called to keep moving in your spiritual journey (*conversatio morum*)?

3   What makes a place 'thin' – as in the Celtic tradition – permeable, as it were, to the divine? What is your experience of going on pilgrimage and encountering holy places of which it might be said 'this is the gate of heaven'?

4   In today's frantic world, we lose a sense of time and place, of sacred space. Globalisation and standardisation mean we may become less attentive to the small picture, the local, the particular and the peculiar. How can we maintain an attentiveness to the local without becoming excessively parochial in outlook? On the other hand, how can we live in solidarity with suffering peoples in different parts of the earth, while remaining rooted in our own locale? What clues do you get from John's gospel?

Prayer exercise

In contemporary times, with smartphones and iPads, we are often one step removed from the natural world, disconnected, literally losing touch with it. So explore with inquisitive eyes your immediate environs. What do you notice? Celebrate the details of your surroundings, environment, setting, context. Appreciate the smallest, tiniest features. Recapture a sense of curiosity. Learn to be intrigued. Give thanks for the incarnate God, the God of the cosmos and the God of the detail.

4

Encountering the fourth dimension: a sense of time

John's gospel reveals a deep paradox about a sense of time. It begins at the very dawn of time: 'In the beginning'. Jesus can talk of being with the Father 'before the foundation of the world' (17:24), sharing glory together in the pre-existent mists of eternity: 'So now, Father, glorify me in your own presence with the glory that I had in your presence before the world existed' (17:5). The Jesus of the fourth gospel can say: 'Before Abraham was, I am' (8:58). Yet alongside this sense of timelessness, the gospel notes the significance of recognising time. Timing is important. At what hour was the centurion's servant healed (4:53)? And everything in the fourth gospel moves towards the fateful and redeeming 'hour'.

With his distinctive perspective on temporality, John wants to *pace* the reader, for the passage of time is celebrated in four distinct phases. First the gospel notes the passage of days. Throughout, there is attentiveness to years, festivals and seasons. During the ponderous last supper discourses, we pause, become contemplative and linger over every word. But then a fast-paced Passion draws us into the very movement and current of Jesus' self-offering, his journey into glorification: we are carried along and swept up into the action.[1]

Days

In the opening narrative, John offers us a succession of days, tumbling after one another with a growing sense of excitement and anticipation that something remarkable is beginning to happen. Our journey starts steadily; time has a momentum, an irresistible thrust forward.

On the first day, John the Baptist gave his testimony about Jesus (1:19–28) at Bethany beyond the Jordan. Then John gives us (italics all mine):

> *The next day* he saw Jesus coming toward him and declared, 'Here is the Lamb of God who takes away the sin of the world.'
> JOHN 1:29

> *The next day* John again was standing with two of his disciples… [Jesus] said to them, 'Come and see.' They came and saw where he was staying, and they remained with him that day. It was about four o'clock in the afternoon.
> JOHN 1:35, 39

> *The next day* Jesus decided to go to Galilee. He found Philip and said to him, 'Follow me.'
> JOHN 1:43

> *On the third day* there was a wedding in Cana of Galilee, and the mother of Jesus was there.
> JOHN 2:1

We have begun a journey: day by day, the action propels us forward. This seems to deliberately evoke the opening verses of Genesis 1, which of course was quoted in the first words of the prologue. There we get an unfolding of creation: 'And there was evening and there was morning, the first day… the second day… the third day.' A new creation is revealing itself in the ministry of Jesus.

Seasons

But from John 2—11, we progress in a steady but reflective way. The whole story spans two years. There is a year from Jesus in Jerusalem with Nicodemus (chapter 2) until the feeding of the multitude (chapter 6):

> The Passover of the Jews was near, and Jesus went up to Jerusalem.
> JOHN 2:13

> When he was in Jerusalem during the Passover festival, many believed in his name because they saw the signs that he was doing.
> JOHN 2:23

> Now the Passover, the festival of the Jews, was near.
> JOHN 6:4

Another year elapses from this event until the meal at Bethany (chapter 12):

> Now the Passover of the Jews was near, and many went up from the country to Jerusalem before the Passover to purify themselves.
> JOHN 11:55

> Six days before the Passover Jesus came to Bethany, the home of Lazarus, whom he had raised from the dead.
> JOHN 12:1

John punctuates the narrative with references to the annual pilgrim feast of Passover. But this, indeed, may be a key John wants us to use to unlock the mystery and meaning of Jesus' death (who, uniquely in John, will be put to death when the Passover lambs are killed – Jesus is the new Passover lamb).

During these two years, John draws our attention to the passage of time as it is marked by other Jewish festivals. Jesus is established as a pilgrim, marking the year's passage in the celebration of feasts.

There is an unnamed festival in Jerusalem (4:45). Later, he will celebrate the Jewish Feast of Tabernacles (7:2, 10). Then comes the Feast of Dedication at Jerusalem, when John notes that 'it was winter' (10:22).

The narrative is punctuated, then, by the rhythm of the festivals, which refers to the passage of the seasons. Each of the festivals has a triple reference: agricultural origins, historical remembrances and eschatological, end-time hopes. In spring, Passover celebrates the barley harvest and recalls the exodus. In the autumn, Tabernacles (the Feast of Booths) celebrates the fruit harvest and the sojourning in tents in Sinai, and looks forward to God enfolding under his canopy all peoples at the end of time. The winter Feast of Dedication (Hanukkah) recalls the rededication of the temple and looks forward to the eschatological light of God.

As Jesus shares in these celebrations, the fourth gospel shows us that he was in touch with the rhythm of the seasons and with mother earth yielding her fruits.

Stillness

A third phase of the gospel slows us right down into a contemplative mode, inviting us to sit with Jesus in the last supper through chapters 13—17. These are the hours of stillness and encroaching darkness. When Judas quits the supper, 'it was night' (13:30).

We have been prepared for this by Jesus' words:

> The light is with you for a little longer. Walk while you have the light, so that the darkness may not overtake you. If you walk

in the darkness, you do not know where you are going. While you have the light, believe in the light, so that you may become children of light.

JOHN 12:35–36

But, in the dark, the words of Jesus illuminate us and radiate hope like candles fluttering in a shadowy room. 'The light shines in the darkness, and the darkness did not overcome it' (1:5).

We are invited to lie with the beloved disciple on the breast of Jesus (13:23). The themes of the discourse call us to a reflective, meditative, contemplative mode of being. We are to slow right down and drink in every word: 'Abide in me as I abide in you' (15:4). The verb *meno* means 'remain', 'stay still', 'settle down', 'reside', 'make your home' (see also 14:23; 15:4–10).

But within this stillness there is a restlessness and a sense of anticipation, a sort of countdown, represented in the phrase 'in a little while':

'A little while, and you will no longer see me, and again a little while, and you will see me.' Then some of his disciples said to one another, 'What does he mean by saying to us, "A little while, and you will no longer see me, and again a little while, and you will see me"; and "Because I am going to the Father"?' They said, 'What does he mean by this "a little while"? We do not know what he is talking about.' Jesus knew that they wanted to ask him, so he said to them, 'Are you discussing among yourselves what I meant when I said, "A little while, and you will no longer see me, and again a little while, and you will see me"? Very truly, I tell you, you will weep and mourn, but the world will rejoice; you will have pain, but your pain will turn into joy.'

JOHN 16:16–20

Hours

As the Passion narrative gets underway, John dramatically increases the tempo.

This has the effect on the reader of being drawn by an unstoppable, irresistible momentum towards the cross, as we allow ourselves to be caught up into the movement of his self-offering: 'I, when I am lifted up from the earth, will draw all people to myself' (12:32).

The arrest of Jesus takes place in the pitch blackness of Gethsemane, suggesting a sense of impending doom. We are told this by the reference to the soldiers and police carrying 'lanterns and torches and weapons' (18:3). It is getting cold. The temperature is dropping fast: 'Now the slaves and the police had made a charcoal fire because it was cold, and they were standing around it and warming themselves. Peter also was standing with them and warming himself' (18:18).

As Jesus faces his accusers in the Jewish court, night is passing, and there are hints of daybreak: 'At that moment the cock crowed' (18:27). John continues: 'Then they took Jesus from Caiaphas to Pilate's headquarters. It was early in the morning' (18:28; 3.00–6.00 am in Roman timing).

John goes on:

> When Pilate heard these words, he brought Jesus outside and sat on the judge's bench at a place called The Stone Pavement, or in Hebrew Gabbatha. Now it was the day of Preparation for the Passover; and it was about noon [lit. the sixth hour]. He said to the Jews, 'Here is your King!'
> JOHN 19:13–14

Jesus dies in late afternoon and is buried at twilight. John is clear:

> Since it was the day of Preparation, the Jews did not want the bodies left on the cross during the sabbath, especially because that sabbath was a day of great solemnity. So they asked Pilate to have the legs of the crucified men broken and the bodies removed.
>
> JOHN 19:31

Three times John tells us it was the day of preparation for the Passover (not the day after, as in the Synoptics). It seems he wants us to realise that Jesus is put to death at the hour the Passover lambs are sacrificed. As Stibbe puts it: 'Here, Christology and chronology are inseparable.'[2]

There follows the sabbath rest of Holy Saturday. It is in the fading blackness of night, just as the sun is rising in the east over the Judean desert and its first rays emerge over the crest of the Mount of Olives, that Mary makes her way to the site: 'Early on the first day of the week, while it was still dark, Mary Magdalene came to the tomb and saw that the stone had been removed from the tomb' (20:1). As Mary herself makes a passage from darkness to light, so the dawn of the new day marks an unforgettable daybreak, the start of the new creation.

Memory

It is a feature of John's chronology that he frequently reminds us of events that have happened in the recent past. It is as if he wants to say to his readers: don't forget – hold on to the memory – it's a vital part of the story, even though we are moving ahead into the future. All of life is interconnected. Do not lose the fragments; all can be gathered up: 'Gather up the fragments left over, so that nothing may be lost' (6:12).

This is a recurrent feature of this gospel. Its function is to suggest that this is not a haphazard series of disconnected events, but everything hangs together, everything belongs and everything has its place. It encourages in the reader a sense of learning to be retrospective, to look back and to recall events in the past that perhaps only now, in the present, begin to make sense.

In John 2, we are told that an enigmatic saying of Jesus begins to make sense only in the reflection that takes place after the resurrection. Jesus had said: 'Destroy this temple, and in three days I will raise it up.' John advises us that 'he was speaking of the temple of his body'. But this realisation comes only with hindsight: 'After he was raised from the dead, his disciples remembered that he had said this; and they believed the scripture and the word that Jesus had spoken' (2:19–22).

In a similar way, the significance of the Palm Sunday event makes sense only in retrospect, in hindsight: 'His disciples did not understand these things at first; but when Jesus was glorified, then they remembered that these things had been written of him and had been done to him' (12:16). Things start to make sense, suggests John, only within a process of recollection and reflection – much in the same way as Zechariah 9:9 is pondered in the light of Easter.

Indeed, John tells us how this process of remembering and reflection takes place. The Holy Spirit brings things to mind, enabling insight, the gaining of perspective and interpretation: 'the Advocate, the Holy Spirit, whom the Father will send in my name, will teach you everything, and remind you of all that I have said to you' (14:26).

John likes to remind us of certain details so that we do not lose them. He offers us an aide-memoire, jogging the memory so we can discern an interconnectedness between events. They are not random or haphazard but are taking place as the Father's will unfolds. For example, as John describes a healing in Cana of Galilee, he reminds us that this was the place of the first sign, the turning of water into wine in chapter 2 (4:46). Later, John tells us: 'He went away again across the Jordan to the place where John had been baptising earlier, and he remained there' (10:40). This serves to remind us of the start of the gospel and the fact that Jesus actually crossed the symbolic Jordan river, pointing back to 1:28.[3]

We can reflect on other examples of flashbacks in the gospel. The visit of the Greeks initially to Philip strikes John as significant because of his Greek hometown: 'They came to Philip, who was from Bethsaida in Galilee, and said to him, "Sir, we wish to see Jesus"' (12:21). This reminds us of 1:44: 'Now Philip was from Bethsaida, the city of Andrew and Peter.' Things are starting to make sense! Another example is in 12:32 – 'When I am lifted up from the earth I will draw all people to myself' – which reminds us of his words to Nicodemus in 3:14.

There is a sense, through the flashbacks in the Passion account, of déjà-vu, or at least the linking of threads that might seem, at first sight, unrelated. There is a sense of fulfilment in Jesus' words of 18:9, with its references back to 17:12 and 10:28–29. In 18:14, John wants to remind us that Caiaphas had prophesied that one man must die for the sake of the whole nation (11:45–53). Significantly, we're told that the manner of Jesus' dying had been indicated by Jesus earlier: a dying that draws all people to himself (18:32): 'This was to fulfil what Jesus had said when he indicated the kind of death he was to die', referring back to 12:32–34.

Finally, we note that 19:39 reminds us that Nicodemus approached Jesus originally in the night hours (3:1–2) – now he is once again making discoveries in the dark. In 21:20, we are told for the third time that the beloved disciple had lain in the breast of Jesus at the last supper (13:23, 25), indicating that this is an important fact that should not be forgotten. All the parts of the mosaic have their significance, and the key, suggests John, lies in the noticing.

As we notice this pacing of time intervals in the fourth gospel and the importance of 'marking time', of using markers for the measurement of time, we are taken aback again and again by John's extraordinary view of time.

The future is now!

Blessings hoped for in the distant future, across the furthest horizon, in the life of the world to come, are actually happening now. We wait no longer. Hope turns to reality.

Approaching the grave of her dead brother Lazarus, Martha reaffirms the traditional and orthodox belief in the age to come: 'I know that he will rise again in the resurrection on the last day' (11:24). But Jesus utters the shattering words: 'I am the resurrection and the life. Those who believe in me, even though they die, will live' (11:25). He had given a clue about these things earlier in his ministry:

> Very truly, I tell you, anyone who hears my word and believes him who sent me has eternal life, and does not come under judgement, but has passed from death to life. Very truly, I tell you, the hour is coming, and is now here, when the dead will hear the voice of the Son of God, and those who hear will live.
> JOHN 5:24–25

The gospel calls us to an alertness to God's work, which can never be predicted or timed. Routine expectations and planning go out of the window: 'Do you not say, "Four months more, then comes the harvest"? But I tell you, look around you, and see how the fields are ripe for harvesting' (4:35). We must not limit God. Human traditions limited what could be done on the sabbath, a 24-hour period of enforced rest. But, in the fourth gospel, Jesus will not be so confined: 'My Father is still working, and I also am working' (5:17).

Eternal life itself is not something we might inherit when we die – it begins right now, in the present moment, when we enter a knowledge of God through Jesus (17:3). It is a quality of life, a dimension of living that we can experience today![4]

'The hour is coming...'

Through Jesus, God is working his purposes out. His ministry does not consist of random events: it represents a destiny unfolding towards the climactic hour. Within the markings of seasons, days and hours, what is vital is the decisive arrival of *the* hour, the day of salvation. Into the progressing *chronos*, the passage of time, breaks the *kairos*, God's timing, the moment that makes all the difference.

In the fourth gospel, this 'hour' of Jesus is a prominent theme in the narrative, a metaphor for the climactic events of Jesus' death and resurrection, which John calls his 'glorification' (12:23; 17:1). Early in the gospel, it is stressed several times that his hour has not yet come (2:4; 7:30; 8:20). In 7:6, he similarly stresses: 'My time has not yet come' (using the Greek word *kairos*).

But it all begins to change with the beginning of the paschal mystery. The account of the last supper begins with these words: 'His hour had come to depart from this world and go to the Father' (13:1). Similarly, in the prayer Jesus addresses to the Father at the end of the last supper discourses, he begins: 'Father, the hour has come; glorify your Son so that the Son may glorify you' (17:1).

Now/not yet

The gospel starts at the dawn of time: 'In the beginning' (1:1). It ends with a tantalising suggestion of the *parousia*: 'until I come' (21:22). John makes other references to the eternal pre-existence of Jesus. To his opponents, Jesus declares: 'Before Abraham was, I am' (8:58). His 'high priestly' prayer refers to a time 'before the foundation of the world' (17:24) and to an era 'before the world existed' (17:5). At one point, Jesus talks about the last day: 'This is indeed the will of my Father, that all who see the Son and believe in him may have eternal life; and I will raise them up on the last day' (6:40).

There is an unresolved tension in John between the 'now' and the 'not yet', the in-breaking work of God in the present and its consummation at the end of time. On the cross, Jesus cries out: 'It is finished.' But it is only just beginning! We live in this tension today, rejoicing in the in-breaking of the kingdom, yet praying 'Your kingdom come'.

. . . .

Spirituality of time

Celebrating the rhythm of day and night

As Philip Newell reminds us, Celtic spirituality was particularly encouraged by the example of John the evangelist. In contrast to the activist Peter, who represents the Roman tradition, the beloved disciple, lying on the breast of Jesus:

> ... had become an image of the practice of listening for the heartbeat of God. The spirituality lent itself to listening for God at the heart of life... The most significant concept to emerge at the Synod of Whitby in 664 was the Celtic mission's perception of John as listening for the heartbeat of God.[5]

So it is appropriate that we turn first of all to see how the Celtic tradition develops a keen sense of time.

In many ways, the Celtic tradition echoes the Johannine sense of time, especially in John's appreciation of light and darkness. In the fourth gospel, night can be seen negatively:

> Jesus answered, 'Are there not twelve hours of daylight? Those who walk during the day do not stumble, because they see the light of this world. But those who walk at night stumble, because the light is not in them.
> JOHN 11:9–10

So, after receiving the piece of bread, [Judas] immediately
went out. And it was night.
JOHN 13:30

That night [the disciples] caught nothing.
JOHN 21:3

We must work the works of him who sent me while it is day;
night is coming when no one can work.
JOHN 9:4

Yet night might also be a time of searching. This is exemplified in
Nicodemus and Mary Magdalene:

Now there was a Pharisee named Nicodemus, a leader of the
Jews. He came to Jesus by night... Nicodemus, who had at first
come to Jesus by night, also came [to the tomb], bringing a
mixture of myrrh and aloes.
JOHN 3:1–2; 19:39

Early on the first day of the week, while it was still dark, Mary
Magdalene came to the tomb and saw that the stone had been
removed from the tomb.
JOHN 20:1

As John affirms in the prologue: 'The light shines in the darkness,
and the darkness did not overcome it' (1:5).

The Celtic tradition celebrates and sanctifies the rhythms of the day.
Esther de Waal puts it:

A people who farmed and knew the pattern of the seasons,
who lived close to the sea and watched the ebb and flow of
tides, above all who watched the daily cycle of the sun and
the changing path of the moon, brought all of this into their
prayer. Here is a way of praying that is essentially holistic. I am

reminded that as a human being living on this earth I am a part
of the pattern of day and night, darkness and light, the waxing
and waning of the moon, the rising and setting of the sun. The
whole of myself is inserted into the rhythm of the elements and
I can here learn something, if I am prepared to, of the ebb and
flow of time and of life itself.[6]

On rising, the Celtic Christian might pray a *lorica* or protection
prayer, such as Patrick's breastplate:

I rise today
with the power of God to pilot me,
God's strength to sustain me,
God's wisdom to guide me,
God's eye to look ahead for me,
God's ear to hear me,
God's word to speak for me,
God's hand to protect me,
God's way before me,
God's shield to defend me

Christ with me, Christ before me, Christ behind me,
Christ within me, Christ beneath me, Christ above me,
Christ to right of me, Christ to left of me;
Christ in my lying, Christ in my sitting, Christ in my rising;
Christ in the heart of all who think of me,
Christ in the tongue of all who speak to me,
Christ in the eye of all who see me,
Christ in the ear of all who hear me.[7]

The anthology *Carmina Gadelica*, prayers collected in the 19th
century in the Hebrides and western Scotland, gives us this *caim* or
circling prayer:

God to enfold me,
God to surround me,
God in my speaking,
God in my thinking.

God in my sleeping,
God in my waking,
God in my watching,
God in my hoping.

God in my life,
God in my lips,
God in my soul,
God in my heart.

God in my sufficing,
God in my slumber,
God in mine ever-living soul,
God in mine eternity.[8]

Celebrating the sacrament of the present moment

In the great classic *Self-Abandonment to Divine Providence*, Jean-Pierre de Caussade (1675–1751) encourages us to abide in a state of surrender to God, welcoming each moment as pregnant with possibilities.[9] De Caussade urged his readers to strive for a synergy, an active cooperation with God's will: 'We know that in all things God works for good for those who love him, who are called according to his purpose' (Romans 8:28, alternative reading). De Caussade believed that God is supremely active in the world, guiding all things according to his divine plans. Our part is to be awake and responsive to God's actions, to allow him to move and direct our life in the midst of change. We are to train ourselves to recognise God's hand of providence in the 'chances and changes of this mortal life'.

De Caussade gave us the striking phrase: 'the sacrament of the present moment'. He teaches us that we should not live in the past nor become anxious about the future, but rather be totally available to God this day and this very moment: 'See, now is the acceptable time; see, now is the day of salvation' (2 Corinthians 6:2). Today, right now, God waits to meet us. De Caussade urges us to live in an attitude of continual surrender to God, yielding ourselves totally to him without qualification or preconditions, so we can become channels through which he can work: 'Loving, we wish to be the instrument of his action so that his love can operate in and through us.'[10] We are to live by humble trust in God, confident that he is working his purposes out. We are to seek not our own fulfilment but God's kingdom:

> Follow your path without a map, not knowing the way, and all will be revealed to you. Seek only God's kingdom and his justice through love and obedience, and all will be granted to you.[11]

Abandoned into God's hands, we are to 'go with the flow' as he opens and closes doors before us.

But what if our prayer resembles Gethsemane, and suffering and upheavals come our way – can these be welcomed as God's will for us? Should we not try to fight against them? De Caussade warns that we must not set bounds or limits to God's plans. He is a 'God of surprises'. He works in unpredictable and unlikely ways and we should be ready for anything: 'The terrifying objects put in our way are nothing. They are only summoned to embellish our lives with glorious adventures.'[12] Hardships can be in God's hands pathways to growth: 'With God, the more we seem to lose, the more we gain. The more he takes from us materially, the more he gives spiritually.'[13] We should not resent difficult circumstances, but rather listen to what God is saying to us through them.

How, then, is it possible to cultivate an attitude of such openness to God? De Caussade affirms that it is achieved by living in communion with God, and allowing Jesus Christ to dwell at the very centre of our being. The Christ who longs to live within us is 'noble, loving, free, serene, and fearless'.[14] De Caussade has a vision of the Christ-life growing within each person who has the courage to surrender to him. This is the secret of recognising 'the sacrament of the present moment'.

A recent writer, Eckhart Tolle, puts it:

> All negativity is caused by an accumulation of psychological time and denial of the present. Unease, anxiety, tension, stress, worry – all forms of fear – are caused by too much future, and not enough presence. Guilt, regret, resentment, grievances, sadness, bitterness, and all forms of non-forgiveness are caused by too much past, and not enough presence.[15]

This resonates with Buddhist teaching on mindfulness, which is enjoying a popular resurgence. Thich Nhat Hanh, for example, teaches that mindfulness is 'keeping one's consciousness alive to the present reality'.[16] It is about becoming present to one's setting in time and space, developing an active awareness and alertness to the present moment, neither regretting the past nor fretting about the future but welcoming and relishing the *now*. It requires an attentiveness to the *now* and avoiding a wandering mind or a dissipated spirit, keeping a calm heart and a focused mind. Slowing down in one's reactions, one learns to breathe more slowly and deeply. Indeed, a certain sensuality is involved, as one is in touch with one's feelings and aware of one's body, posture and in particular the movement of inhalation and exhalation of breath. In Buddhist thought, such wakefulness to the present moment is inseparable from the practice of compassion towards those around you. In Christian terms, we might say that meditation leads to mediation, contemplation to courageous action.

. . . .

Questions for reflection

1 In what ways do you mark and celebrate the passing of time, during the day, week, year? How can this make a difference to approaching the realities of ageing?

2 How do you find yourself responding to John's call, in the last supper discourses, to slow right down and enter a contemplative mode? What difference might this make to daily living?

3 What rises in your heart when you think of the future? Name your hopes and fears.

4 What are you learning from John's gospel about approaches to time? The Johannine tradition goes on to affirm Christ as the Alpha and Omega. What strikes you in John's approach as being most significant to your own life?

Prayer exercise

Either
On a clean piece of paper, draw a personal 'timeline' to recall the transitions you have faced in your life. Draw a horizontal line and mark it into the decades of your life. Above the line, note major events and transitions, including new jobs, house moves, births and deaths, new ministries. Below the line, try to note how you felt at these moments of change. How did you experience God at these moments? If in a group setting, you might like to reflect on this with a partner. Bring this to a close by giving thanks for God's providence in your life, and entrust your future to him.

Or

Make a careful review of the previous day as in the tradition of the Ignatian *examen*, which we will look at in the next chapter. Recall what things happened, whom you met (whether intended or 'accidentally'), what you did. Was Christ calling you in a way that you did not recognise at the time? Did you hear his voice – or miss it? Did you obey? How did you handle interruptions or unexpected challenges? Did you find yourself resenting any task? Be penitent for negative attitudes or opportunities missed. Praise God for the times you were aware of his presence. Then take time to pray for a greater awareness of his presence today, and watch how God can bring people across your path and speak to you in unexpected ways and through unlikely individuals. Be ready to have your best-laid plans interrupted and stay open to God's surprises. Pray for a rediscovery of a sense of 'providence'.

5

Feeling intensity, touching infinity

In this chapter, we explore two key, interrelated themes: the senses of touch and feeling. John's gospel leads us into a deeper appreciation not only of the physicality and emotionality of the Word made flesh, but also of the importance of these dimensions in our own spirituality and discipleship. Learning from Jesus in the fourth gospel, we will rediscover ourselves.

Jesus touches

Throughout, the fourth gospel makes many allusions to the sense of touch. There are 30 references to touch in relation to fingers, hands and feet.

In his ministry we see Jesus:

- in the temple forecourts, gripping a whip of cords, lifting up and smashing down to the ground the tables of the money changers
- twice writing with his finger in the dust
- applying a lotion made of spittle and mud to the eyes of the man born blind.

Sensations and textures are evoked by the narrative:

- the cool shade of the fig tree enjoyed by Nathaniel
- the cushioning grass of the hillside where people sit down
- the feel of water poured over dusty feet
- the chill of the night of the Passion

- a shivering Peter warming himself by the fire 'because it was cold' (18:18)
- the fresh dew of Easter morning in the garden
- the cold, hard slab of the tomb
- the bracing water against Peter's tingling naked skin as he jumps into the lake to swim to Jesus.

Violent touch

In the Passion story, John makes references to violent touch – physical clash, collision, conflict. Jesus' enemies want to lay hands on him in order to arrest him (7:30, 44; 10:39). Blows are laid on him; he is hit by the hands of the high priest's servants and by the soldiers and feels the sting of pain in his face:

> When [Jesus] had said this, one of the police standing nearby struck Jesus on the face, saying, 'Is that how you answer the high priest?' Jesus answered… 'If I have spoken rightly, why do you strike me?'
> JOHN 18:22–23

Then he feels ropes or chains fastened to his wrists as 'Annas sent him bound to Caiaphas the high priest' (18:24). Pilate orders men to take whips into their hands to flog and lash Jesus (19:1). During this ordeal, 'they kept coming up to him, saying, "Hail, King of the Jews!" and striking him on the face' (19:3). Jesus feels the thorns pierce his brow and, after bearing the crushing weight of the cross on his shoulders, he will receive the nails of crucifixion.

Tender touch

Yet also in the narrative leading up to the Passion, John offers us glimpses of tenderest touch. We read of:

- the anointing of Jesus' feet by Mary with the aromatic oils. Maybe they tickle as she wipes his feet with her hair (chapter 12).

- the foot-washing, where Jesus holds in his hands the dusty feet of the disciples, pours water and wipes them lovingly with a towel (chapter 13)
- the beloved disciple lying on the breast of Jesus, which is mentioned three times (13:23, 25; 21:20) so this is not accidental but in some way significant.

But in the accounts of Easter, there seems at first sight to be a contradiction in connection with the sense of touch. To Thomas, Jesus says beckoningly: 'Put your finger here' (20:27). But to Mary Magdalene, the risen Christ says firmly: 'Do not hold on to me' (20:17; 'Touch me not', KJV). Thomas is invited to touch the very wounds of Christ, but Mary is instructed to back off. What are we to make of this paradox?

The touch of Mary Magdalene: spurned?

> She turned round and saw Jesus standing there, but she did not know that it was Jesus. Jesus said to her, 'Woman, why are you weeping? For whom are you looking?' Supposing him to be the gardener, she said to him, 'Sir, if you have carried him away, tell me where you have laid him, and I will take him away.' Jesus said to her, 'Mary!' She turned and said to him in Hebrew, 'Rabbouni!' (which means Teacher). Jesus said to her, 'Do not hold on to me, because I have not yet ascended to the Father. But go to my brothers and say to them, "I am ascending to my Father and your Father, to my God and your God."'
> JOHN 20:14–17

Noli me tangere, meaning 'Don't touch me', is the Latin version of the words spoken and becomes the title of famous artistic depictions of the event. In Titian's painting (c. 1514), it looks as if Jesus recoils from her. In Fra Angelico's attempt (1442), Jesus walks away from her. Correggio (1525) creates a gaping void between Jesus and the Magdalene.

The form of the verb used is not the aorist imperative, which would indicate momentary action, but the present, which indicates an ongoing action in progress. The original Greek phrase (*mē mou haptou*) is better represented in translation as 'cease holding on to me' or 'stop clinging to me'. It strongly suggests that Mary has already begun an embrace or touch with Christ, but this cannot be allowed to go on indefinitely. Perhaps it is best rendered: 'Don't grasp, don't clutch or grip me.' Or more bluntly: 'Don't clasp me possessively; let me go!' Jesus is on the loose. He, the transcendent one, can't be held down. In Matthew and Mark's accounts, he is off to Galilee. In John, he is off to heaven. There is no holding him down: she has to let him go. Later, we will notice possible allusions to the Song of Songs in the resurrection account. There, Gregory of Nyssa sees a powerful allegory of the relationship between God (the bridegroom) and the Christian (the bride). The bridegroom is a dynamic figure, ever in movement: 'Look, he comes, leaping upon the mountains, bounding over the hills. My beloved is like a gazelle' (Song of Songs 2:8–9). He is off!

The touch of Thomas: demanded?

> So the other disciples told [Thomas], 'We have seen the Lord.' But he said to them, 'Unless I see the mark of the nails in his hands, and put my finger in the mark of the nails and my hand in his side, I will not believe.' A week later his disciples were again in the house, and Thomas was with them. Although the doors were shut, Jesus came and stood among them and said, 'Peace be with you.' Then he said to Thomas, 'Put [Gr. *balein*, lit. 'thrust'] your finger here and see my hands. Reach out your hand and put it in my side. Do not doubt but believe.' Thomas answered him, 'My Lord and my God!'
> JOHN 20:25–28

Thomas is permitted to explore with his very fingertips the sacred and scarred body of Christ. He is invited to touch in order to verify, identify, clarify. This resonates with Luke's account, where he must prove he is no ghost or apparition:

He said to them, 'Why are you frightened, and why do doubts arise in your hearts? Look at my hands and my feet; see that it is I myself. Touch me and see; for a ghost does not have flesh and bones as you see that I have.' And when he had said this, he showed them his hands and his feet.

LUKE 24:37–40

In John, Thomas is permitted to touch the very wounds of Jesus in order to confirm his identity and continuity – that it really is the same Jesus he knew before, not an apparition or dream. But he will not keep on holding on. He will release Jesus!

Touched by the breath of God

In John 20:19, the disciples experience the nausea and claustrophobia of being locked up together in the upper room, 'for fear'. They experience the stuffiness, the heat, the confinement that become for the evangelist a symbol of the captivity of the soul. Yet Jesus appears and, breathing in and out, he feels his lungs expand in a physical sensation which at once is a profoundly spiritual moment. John puts it concisely: 'He breathed on them and said to them, "Receive the Holy Spirit"' (20:22). Evoking the Spirit's breath in the coming to life of man in the very beginning, 'the breath of life' (Genesis 2:7), Jesus is initiating a new creation. The disciples remember that, at the dawn of creation, Genesis tells us that the wind of God blew over the primal chaos of the waters. They might recall the divine promise spoken in the valley of dry bones: 'I will cause breath to enter you, and you shall live' (Ezekiel 37:5). As the disciples feel the cooling breath of Jesus on their skin and in their souls, they experience an empowerment beyond words. 'Breathe on me, breath of God, fill me with life anew!' (Edwin Hatch, 1878). The episode in the upper room reminds us that the wind or breath of God is utterly indispensable.

Wind in our faces, blowing in the soul

This is a theme that John introduced near the beginning of the gospel: 'The wind blows where it chooses, and you hear the sound of it, but you do not know where it comes from or where it goes. So it is with everyone who is born of the Spirit' (John 3:8).

Jesus is inviting us to recognise in the very air around us the mystery of God's workings. The Holy Spirit, like the gusting wind, is ineffable and unknowable but *felt*. He is invisible yet omnipresent. The Spirit, like the wind, might also turn out to be unpredictable, uncontrollable, disturbing, a risky element to be exposed to: 'The lake became rough because a strong wind was blowing' (6:18).

John knows well the winds of Palestine, its gentle breezes and stormy gales. What type of wind buffeting us does he have in mind when he writes of the unseen wind? The cooling afternoon breeze that blows in from the Mediterranean, bringing refreshment? The dry scorching Hamsin wind gusting from the south that unsettles? The stormy wet winter wind, which comes as the harbinger of spring, turning back the drought and enabling new shoots? At various points in our lives, the Holy Spirit will come to us differently. We may not predict the moving of the wind in our spiritual lives, but we must expose ourselves to its presence. We need to stay alert and decide whether it is time to hoist the sails, catch the wind and follow the leading of the Spirit – or whether it is time to take cover!

Gerard Manley Hopkins (1844–89) develops the metaphor in daring ways in his poem 'The blessed virgin compared to the air we breathe'. He calls her:

> *Wild air, world-mothering air,*
> *Nestling me everywhere.*[1]

Wind – and air – become for John, too, powerful images of God's providence and mysterious presence.

'Daily we touch him'

Can we touch the risen Christ? Daily we touch him… in four ways, at least!

Touch him in the sacraments

In the sacraments, through 'outward and visible signs of inward and invisible grace',[2] God touches us and energises us. We feel the cascade of the Holy Spirit, drenching and inundating us in the waters of baptism. In some traditions, we might then receive Chrismation – an anointing with the fragrant and rich oil of chrism, by which the sign of the cross, traced on our foreheads, marks us out as Christians.

In broken bread and poured-out wine, we feel in our hand and on our tongue a sign of the presence of Christ. In the Eucharist, we also offer to one another hands of welcome and acceptance, greeting Christ in one another in the sign of the peace. We touch Christ, not in order to cling or grasp, but to verify, appreciate and welcome his very presence. We take Christ into our hands, and upon our lips, in order to share him with others.

In the sacrament of healing, we receive on our broken and bruised bodies an anointing with holy oil, which communicates restoring grace to wounded hearts and crushed spirits.

Touch him in the sacrament of creation

We have already considered the theme of encountering God in creation. In one of the recommended prayer exercises at the end of this chapter, you are invited to pray with your fingertips, caressing and stroking the divine in the surfaces of the natural world, enjoying a prayer that is tangible and tactile.

Touch him in the sacrament of the poor

In Matthew 25:34–40, Jesus tells us that when you feed the hungry and clothe the naked, 'just as you did it to one of the least of these who are members of my family, you did it to me' – you touched Jesus. Where do we find God? Where should we be looking for Christ? Can it be that we can encounter him in the broken lives of the oppressed?

> Then the king will say to those at his right hand, 'Come, you that are blessed by my Father; inherit the kingdom prepared for you from the foundation of the world, for I was hungry and you gave me food, I was thirsty and you gave me something to drink, I was a stranger and you welcomed me, I was naked and you gave me clothing, I was sick and you took care of me, I was in prison and you visited me… Truly I tell you, just as you did it to one of the least of those who are members of my family, you did to me.'
>
> MATTHEW 25:34–36, 40

This Jesus invites us to find him in 'these brothers and sisters of mine' who are hungry, broken, stripped, imprisoned, estranged. The incarnation overturns the traditional dichotomy between sacred and secular, the divide between 'holy' and 'unholy'. It challenges us to glimpse the divine in the dust, and to be alert to God's presence in the broken.[3] It alerts us to the possibility that Christ might be close at hand, incognito, waiting to be recognised and greeted with a touch of love. As we learn to discern the features of Jesus in the faces of those who suffer, we realise that we touch him in the lives of the broken, where he waits to meet us.

Touch him in contemplation

Thomas Merton writes:

> Contemplation knows God by seeming to touch him. Or rather it knows him as if it had been invisibly touched by him…

Touched by him who has no hands, but who is pure Reality and the source of all that is real! Hence contemplation is a sudden gift of awareness, an awakening to the Real within all that is real. A vivid awareness of infinite Being at the roots of our own limited being. An awareness of our contingent reality as received, as a present from God, a free gift of love. This is the existential contact of which we speak when we use the metaphor of being 'touched by God.'[4]

Feel

Touch and feel are inseparable. Physical sensations received by touch resonate in the soul. When we say 'we are touched', we are referring to an inner emotional state that stirs deep within. As we celebrate the humanity and physicality of Christ, we realise afresh that he was a passionate and full-bloodied human revealing the deepest intensities of the soul. This is indeed a recurrent theme in the fourth gospel. Stephen Voorwinde reminds us:

> Of the 60 specific references to the emotions of Jesus in the gospels, 28 are found in John. More so than the other gospels, John offers a close-up picture of Jesus' life and ministry… John's portrayal of Jesus' emotions is unique among the four gospel accounts.[5]

There are five emotions that are prominent.

1 Burning passion

In John 2, we get a glimpse into a heart on fire. As Jesus encounters the temple precincts turned into a marketplace and the grasping money changers extracting extortionate exchange rates from pilgrims paying the temple tax, we see a forceful and uncompromising reaction: he overturns tables, pours the coins on to the ground and, making a whip of cords, drives out both animals and men. We might glimpse a righteous anger and indignation, but that is not how the disciples remember the event. They recall a text from Psalm 69:9, which for them encapsulates Jesus' emotions in this moment: 'Zeal for your house will consume me.' Jesus is eaten up with a passion: for the verse in Psalms, the CEV gives us: 'My love for your house burns in me like a fire,' while TLB puts it: 'My zeal for God and his work burns hot within me.' For *The Message* this is: 'I love you more than I can say. Because I'm madly in love with you.' Jesus is possessed by a zeal, an energy, an intense longing for the purity and purpose of the temple and what it stands for. He is no 'gentle Jesus, meek and mild'!

In his debate with Jewish religious authorities in John 8, we witness a combative and feisty Jesus. He is infuriated. He does not mince his words into theological niceties and pleasantries. He calls a spade a spade: 'You are from your father the devil, and you choose to do your father's desires. He was a murderer from the beginning… He is a liar and the father of lies' (8:44). Jesus again speaks with passion and deepest longing: 'If the Son makes you free, you will be free indeed' (8:36). His heart is at once disturbed by the complacency of his opponents yet brimming over with concern and yearning for them.

2 Practical compassion

Again and again, John gives us a glimpse into the patient, practical compassion of Jesus. He displays great solicitude for those who are marginalised, excluded and cast out. At Samaria's well, he sits down next to the ostracised woman who is evidently judged harshly by her own community. She certainly is a woman with some experience, but Jesus sees her as worthy of receiving and bearing the life-giving water of the Spirit. In his words to her, he celebrates her potential and her possibilities. He transforms her life by empowering one who was a nobody into being evangelist to the entire town.

At Bethesda's pool, Jesus likewise recognises and releases potential and possibility where everyone else sees a problem. He notices the lame man who is gripped by an inner paralysis of fatalism and has been ill for an astonishing 38 years (5:6). He responds not with a 'There, there!' sympathy but with an empowering command: 'Stand up, take your mat and walk.' This is compassion with an edge – tough love!

In John 9, Jesus notices a man and fiercely contradicts the opinion of the disciples that his incapacity is punishment for his parents' or his own sin. As we noted, in sending him down to the Pool of Siloam, a public *mikveh* or immersion pool for dusty pilgrims arriving in the holy city from the desert, Jesus restores his very life purpose: to be a pilgrim with a welcome place in God's temple. All his life, he had been excluded from the sanctuary: now, Jesus' compassion revolutionises the man's life and gives him new dignity and a fresh future.

In the fourth gospel, we see the compassion and longing of Jesus. There is a poignancy and sensitivity in his promise to the disciples at the last supper: 'I will not leave you orphaned' (14:18). The AMPC spells it out: 'I will not leave you as orphans [comfortless, desolate, bereaved, forlorn, helpless]; I will come [back] to you.' Alluding to his coming death, he knows that this will be experienced as a shocking wrench and loss. Brimming with compassion, he promises a Comforter, another advocate, a counsellor, a divine consoling and energising presence (14:16).

3 Heart-rending anguish

John uses extraordinarily strong and powerful verbs to express the inner turmoil of Jesus. Three episodes stand out.

At the tomb of Lazarus
John gives us deep insight into the emotions of Jesus, in his narrative of chapter 11: 'When Jesus saw Mary weeping, and the Jews who came with her also weeping, he was greatly disturbed in spirit and deeply moved' (11:33). The word 'troubled' (Greek: *enebrimesato*) is almost impossible to translate. It denotes the snorting of horses and the release of suppressed rage or indignation. The KJV gives us: 'He

groaned in the spirit, and was troubled'; from the GNT we have: 'His heart was touched, and he was deeply moved.' But the JUB gives us a stronger rendering: 'He became enraged in the Spirit and stirred himself up.' The WYC puts it: 'He made noise in spirit.'

After Jesus sheds tears – 'Jesus began to weep' (11:35) – this extraordinary verb is repeated by John from verse 33. In 11:38, *The Message* gives us: 'Then Jesus, the anger again welling up within him, arrived at the tomb.' TLB puts it: 'Again Jesus was moved with deep anger' while the AMPC suggests: 'Now Jesus, again sighing repeatedly and deeply disquieted, approached the tomb.'

What might be the cause of his anger or exasperation? Is Jesus perturbed by the faithless wailing of the Jews? Is he responding to 'Mary's profound grief and the moaning and weeping of her companions' (11:33, *The Voice*)? Is he pained by the ugliness and stench of death itself, or by the foreboding that suggests to him his own impending death? John draws attention to the depth of feeling by referring to his being moved 'in spirit'. One thing is clear: Jesus does not linger in this moment of grief. He is impelled into action. He calls his friend Lazarus out from the tomb without further delay, believing that this will be another opportunity to turn human drama into an outbreak of divine glory – as he had said to Martha: 'Did I not tell you that if you believed, you would see the glory of God?' (11:40).

In his encounter with Greeks
Here, Jesus is described as being 'troubled' (12:27). The word employed in the passive tense (Greek: *tetaraktai*) literally means 'shaken together' or 'stirred up' and is used in this sense in 5:7 in reference to the waters being disturbed. Jesus is disturbed, thrown into confusion. Different translations shed light on the shades of meaning. The ISV gives us: 'Now my soul is in turmoil' while J.B. Phillips renders this poignantly as: 'Now comes my hour of heartbreak.' For *The Message*, this emerges as: 'Right now I am stormtossed. And what am I going to say? "Father, get me out of this"?' *The Voice* places on Jesus' lips: 'My spirit is low and unsettled.' The NOG

suggests: 'I am too deeply troubled now to know how to express my feelings. Should I say, "Father, save me from this time of suffering"? No! I came for this time of suffering.'

But Jesus is uninhibited. He freely and unreservedly expresses his inner feelings. He releases into the external world his inner turmoil. There is an echo of Jeremiah's experience, who speaks of an inner flame, a divine compulsion: 'If I say, "I will not mention him, or speak any more in his name", then within me there is something like a burning fire shut up in my bones; I am weary with holding it in, and I cannot' (Jeremiah 20:9). After Jesus' soul-wrenching conflict in 12:27, the narrative goes on: 'Jesus cried aloud...' (12:44).

At the last supper
The same powerful verb is repeated here. As he announces his imminent betrayal, Jesus is once again troubled (13:21; Greek: *etarachthe*) but this time the evangelist adds a further dimension: 'troubled in spirit'. In his inmost being, Jesus was being torn apart. He was burning with love for the disciples (13:1), yet he was wounded bitterly in soul as he saw this love being spurned and rejected by one of his chosen men. Though this is an inner pain, translators emphasise its outward aspects: for *The Message*: 'Jesus became visibly upset'; for *The Voice*: 'Jesus was becoming visibly distressed.'

4 Infectious joy

All this forms a dramatic contrast with the joy Jesus exudes and speaks of regularly in the fourth gospel. Indeed, the joy and pain are intermingled and inseparable as in the experience of a woman's childbirth:

> Very truly, I tell you, you will weep and mourn, but the world will rejoice; you will have pain, but your pain will turn into joy. When a woman is in labour, she has pain, because her hour has come. But when her child is born, she no longer remembers the anguish because of the joy of having brought a human being

into the world. So you have pain now; but I will see you again, and your hearts will rejoice, and no one will take your joy from you.

JOHN 16:20–22

This is the second allusion to childbirth in the fourth gospel for, at the outset, when Jesus is looking for a metaphor with which to communicate the foundational spiritual experience of conversion, he refers to a birth by water and the spirit (John 3).

Frequently in John's gospel, Jesus speaks of a God-given joy bringing a sense of completion, fulfilment or wholeness. Speaking of the Baptist, he testifies: 'He who has the bride is the bridegroom. The friend of the bridegroom, who stands and hears him, rejoices greatly at the bridegroom's voice. For this reason my joy has been fulfilled' (3:29). In the midst of the last supper discourse, Jesus alludes to a paschal joy that will come with his glorification on the cross and the gift of the Spirit: 'I have said these things to you so that my joy may be in you, and that your joy may be complete' (15:11); 'Until now you have not asked for anything in my name. Ask and you will receive, so that your joy may be complete' (16:24). In his high-priestly prayer, he says to the Father: 'But now I am coming to you, and I speak these things in the world so that they may have my joy made complete in themselves' (17:13). He speaks of a full measure or perfection of joy.

In addition to these specific references, there is an underground stream of humour beneath the fourth gospel, which bubbles up unexpectedly, here and there. One can glimpse a smile on Jesus' face and even his laughter in the joyous moments like the extravagant wine at Cana's wedding and the reunion over breakfast in John 21. There is certainly an undercurrent of humour in the narratives concerning the Samaritan woman (John 4) and the healing of the man born blind and its aftermath (John 9).[6]

5 Outreaching love

While there are just four references to love in Mark's gospel, eleven in Matthew and twelve in Luke, there are an astonishing 39 references in the fourth gospel. This is summed up in 13:1: 'Having loved his own who were in the world, he loved them to the end' – to the uttermost, the furthest limit. As *The Voice* renders this: 'From beginning to end, Jesus' days were marked by His love for His people.'

We see this love expressed in acceptance of the wounded and fragile, represented in the Samaritan woman and the man born blind. Particular people are singled out for affection: Mary, Martha and Lazarus (11:5) and of course the one designated the 'beloved disciple'. In Peter's restoration (21:15–19), Jesus looks for a reciprocal, answering love that responds to his acceptance. While the love of Jesus reveals itself in tenderness and embrace of the other – welcoming the beloved disciple to put his head on his very breast, allowing the woman to bathe his feet with her tears – this love is no sentimentality. It is characterised by God's pre-eminent approach to the cosmos: 'For God so loved the world that he gave his only Son, so that everyone who believes in him may not perish but may have eternal life' (3:16). Love is measured by self-giving and sacrifice: 'This is my commandment, that you love one another as I have loved you. No one has greater love than this, to lay down one's life for one's friends' (15:12–13).

Though John is explicit about some of the feelings of Christ, there remains an ellusiveness, an unsolvable enigma about them. Culpepper puts it:

> There remains a 'heart of darkness' in the character of Jesus in the sense that the central mystery is never quite penetrated, never fully exposed. Like most good plots and all good characters, John and its Jesus retain areas of shadow and mystery it will not illuminate for the reader.[7]

Voorwinde cautions us against too quickly assigning the emotions to the humanity of Jesus:

> To understand the emotions of Jesus in the fourth gospel, it is not sufficient to place them in 'human' or 'divine' categories… [They] often gain their significance as well as their poignancy in the interplay of Jesus' roles as the covenant Lord and the covenant sacrifice.[8]

It is John's conviction that Jesus reveals to the world the heart of the Father: 'No one has ever seen God. It is God the only Son, who is close to the Father's heart, who has made him known' (1:18). The one who in eternity lies on the Father's bosom invites a beloved disciple to place his head on his, in a symbol of tender acceptance and attentive listening. Jesus describes friendship in terms of sharing intimate knowledge with close confidants: 'I have called you friends, because I have made known to you everything that I have heard from my Father' (15:15). In another place (10:30), Jesus declares: 'The Father and I are one.'

In his gospel, John is leading us to understand the Father's heart, through the Word made flesh. He is saying: 'This is the sort of God I believe in: I believe in a kind of God who feels, not an impassible Word[9] but one of whom it can be said, "God so loved the world". My God cherishes, delights in and feels for humanity.' In the emotions of Jesus, as John uniquely reveals them to us, we glimpse a God in solidarity with the hurting and the vulnerable, not forgetting a God in joyous communion with those who enjoy good wine. Jesus' revealed and expressed feelings give us permission, if we need it, to express our emotions honestly and 'from the heart', and not hold back.

· · · · · · · · · · · · · · · · · ·

Spirituality of touch

Franciscan spirituality gives us an inspiring example of a spirituality that reaches the divine through touch. As we reflect on the life of Francis of Assisi, we recall how he shows us how our very hands can be used, for good or ill:

- **Wielding**: As a young soldier, Francis found himself brandishing weapons to be used in conflict with the neighbouring city state of Perugia.
- **Fighting**: Clenched fists were used in hand-to-hand combat, for punching, slapping and striking.
- **Grasping**: As a young man working in his father's shop, Francis was eager to exact maximum profits from his customers as he sold them the latest fashions in cloth.
- **Relinquishing**: As his conversion got underway, Francis literally released his grip on material things, stripping off his very clothes before his father, and dropping a bag of coins before the priest.
- **Shaping**: Hearing the call 'Rebuild my church', Francis initially took this literally as he assembled rocks to repair ruined chapels.
- **Receiving**: Francis took into his hands the Word of Life, the book of the gospel, as a deacon called to proclaim the good news in church and out of it.
- **Reaching out**: Francis felt impelled to touch the untouchable and to embrace the leper he encountered on the road. He later wrote: 'What was nauseating to me became sweetness' (*Testament*).
- **Welcoming**: At Gubbio, he held in his arms the head of the hated wolf that the townsfolk were trying to stone to death.
- **Celebrating**: Francis reached out joyously to the elements of creation, as in his song the 'Canticle of Creation', making a physical and reverent connection with sister water and brother wind and mother earth.
- **Greeting**: At Damietta, Francis quit the Crusaders' military camp besieging the Islamic town. He crossed several barriers and walls, and went in to greet the Muslim sultan, with whom he spent days in listening and witnessing.

- **Exalting**: He lifted up his hands in praise and worship to God his creator.
- **Sharing**: Francis recklessly gave away all he had, time and again, even the clothes on his back and the breviary.

Towards the end of his life, Francis' hands were honoured by God in a singular way as, in 1224 on Mount Alverna, he received in his palms and feet the stigmata, signs of the very wounds of Christ on the cross. His hands had become, literally, Christlike: wounded, vulnerable, but ready to give out and touch, healing and reconciling.

Look at your hands. How will you use them today to communicate the love of Christ? How will you touch the divine today?

Spirituality of feelings

The gift of tears

John's gospel gives a prominent place to tears.[10] Four times in John 11, reference is made to weeping:

> They followed her because they thought that she was going to the tomb to weep there... When Jesus saw her weeping, and the Jews who came with her also weeping, he was greatly disturbed in spirit and deeply moved... Jesus began to weep.
> JOHN 11:31, 33, 35

This is a powerful anticipation of his promise at the last supper: 'Very truly, I tell you, you will weep and mourn, but the world will rejoice; you will have pain, but your pain will turn into joy' (16:20). In the Easter garden, tears flow readily: 'Mary stood weeping outside the tomb. As she wept, she bent over to look into the tomb' (20:11). Twice the question is put, first by angels and second by Jesus: 'Woman, why are you weeping?' (20:13, 15). Indeed, what do the tears signify?

In his homily on Ash Wednesday 2015, Pope Francis encouraged Catholics to ask God for 'the gift of tears in order to make our prayer and our journey of conversion more authentic and without hypocrisy'. It is the Orthodox tradition that celebrates the gift of tears as a particular grace from God. As Bishop Kallistos Ware puts it:

> When it is genuinely spiritual 'speaking with tongues' seems to represent an act of 'letting go' – the crucial moment in the breaking down of our sinful self-trust, and its replacement by a willingness to allow God to act with us. In the Orthodox tradition this act of 'letting go' more often takes the form of the gift of tears.[11]

The gift of weeping can denote utter surrender into God's hands, a sign of vulnerability and susceptibility to God, a dissolving of our self-protective barriers that fence us off from the divine. They may express *penthos* – compunction, penitence. Indeed, the Fathers often speak of tears in two senses: as a sign of sorrow for sin, and as a sign of joy at the recognition of one's salvation (see, for example, the treatise of St Theognetus in the *Philokalia*). St Isaac the Syrian puts it:

> Tears are proof that the human soul has won divine mercy. It has been accepted by God through repentance and has now entered upon the phase of purity.

St Photios speaks of the fountain of tears:

> That most excellent and most beneficial blessing which drips down the cheeks, yet washing splendidly the soul… and waters the garden of our souls to bear fruits for us.

The Orthodox tradition suggests that such tears are a renewal of the cleansing of baptism: indeed, St Gregory of Nazianzus coined the expression 'baptism of tears'. St Basil the Great encourages us to seek the gift of tears:

If you wish to wash your face, wash it, flood it with tears so that it may shine with glory before God and his holy angels. A face bathed with tears has an un-withering beauty.[12]

The gift of feelings

Patterns of spirituality developed by Ignatius of Loyola help us to get in touch with our feelings and responses to God, in order to discern God's call to us. What do you really want? Ignatian prayer practices uncover the deepest desires of the human heart. Typically, these are smothered by superficial desires for transitory things. Our most profound desires are shaped by the Holy Spirit and point towards new choices for spiritual growth and fruitful service.

We are invited to move from shallow, superficial and surface desires to naming the deep desire in our heart, which resonates with 'the fundamental principle', what we were created for: 'Man has been created to praise, reverence and serve our Lord God, thereby saving his soul' (23).[13] While it is not always helpful or even possible to work out where a desire has come from, Ignatius suggests that we might detect where we sense our desire is leading, naming the direction in which it is pointing.

Our deepest desires coalesce and crystallise in a clear sense of our vocation. We realise that our yearnings meet God's longings for us. We each have a unique song to sing. We each have a singular God-given vocation and meaning in life. God calls us into a particular role to play in his mission.[14] The Ignatian tradition[15] reminds us: God is present in all human experience; God is a self-communicating God; God can be experienced in our hearts, minds, imaginations, psyches and bodies; God communicates Self to us in a personal way; God waits and longs for us to respond. Our brokenness, sinfulness, blindness and other areas of captivity can prevent us from noticing and responding to God's self-communication. God desires that we be healed, made whole and more completely human and alive. Ignatian prayer recognises God's specific self-communication in life, prayer and relationships. It savours, relives and enjoys the deep affective touches of God. We seek to respond both interiorly and exteriorly to God's self-revelation. We notice differences in ourselves as a result of affective experiences of God.

We need not only to be awake and alert to our true feelings but also to be able to discern what God is saying through our feelings, reading them in the light of the Spirit. Here, Ignatius' distinction between consolations and desolations alerts us to what God is saying to us in our prayers. Despite their names, they do not necessarily represent happy feelings or sad feelings, but rather what leads to God and the service of others, and what leads away from God and from others. A consolation might be happy – a sense of being blessed by God – or it might be, for example, a feeling of penitence or brokenness, which leads us back to God's grace. A 'dark night of the soul' could turn out to be a consolation because it leads to a greater awareness of God. A desolation might indeed be a bleak experience, but it could also be enjoyable in a self-centred or narcissistic way, so it leads away from God and from others. The devil appears as an angel of light; a 'feel-good' factor might actually turn out to be a desolation.

In Ignatius' approach, we articulate both our feelings and our reactions in prayer, and recognise what this is telling us not only about ourselves but also about what God may be saying to us. We need to ask questions like: is this leading me towards greater courage, greater solidarity with hurting ones? Ignatius says of consolations: 'This is the name I give to any interior movement experienced in the soul, causing it to glow with love' (316). Anything that leads to an increase of faith, hope or love can be celebrated and welcomed as a consolation. He also gives a range of examples of feelings to be recognised as desolations: where the soul finds itself listless, apathetic, tepid, lacking confidence.

Ignatius encourages us to be responsive to what he calls 'interior movements' (316) – movements in the soul, shifts in perception, transitions, inner changes. He says: 'We should pay great attention to the entire train of thought. If beginning, middle and end are wholly sound, tending to what is completely innocent, this is a sign of the good angel' (333). A key Ignatian word is 'noticing' – spotting the signs.

A vital exercise for daily use is Ignatius' *examen*,[16] which can become a great stimulus for discernment. We make a prayerful review of each day and ask such questions as: What were the creative moments? What were hurtful or life-denying? As we replay some of the key moments and revisit the experiences, we reconnect with the feelings produced and begin to sift and sort them. We pray for enlightenment about any particular moments that stand out in our recent memory, especially if they reveal a shift of mood or feeling. We ask God to show us where these feelings came from – from God or somewhere else? Where was God in these experiences, and what is he saying to me now about them? This is not an exercise in introspection but a seeking of God's light to shine on our day, with a deep concern that we have fulfilled God's mission in some way. We close by celebrating and giving thanks for God's presence in us through the day and for working through us, even if we were not aware of it at the time, but only in hindsight. This exercise is not, then, about making our own analysis or of judgement on the 'success' of the day but rather it is about becoming more alert to God's movement in us. We might conclude the exercise by entrusting the coming day to God, with the particular intention that we will be alert to his call, however it comes – and it often comes through the needs of others.

By alertness to our feelings, we start to notice what is important and what is not. We begin to spot and give name to God's nudging. Our vocation, springing from our baptismal call to share in God's mission, begins to clarify. We become aware of what God is asking of us. We see in greater focus our priorities as Christians. We become more alert to our strengths and weakness. We are able to recognise and celebrate our spiritual gifts. This journey of discernment unlocks and releases undiscovered, latent or hidden talents for the sake of God's mission in the world. We discover total availability to God. And, as we reflect on our own identity and calling, we realise that every person has spiritual potential to be nurtured and, made in the image of God, a capacity for the divine. As we gain a fresh sense of our own selfhood in God, we discover an understanding of human destiny and capacity for God – a theological anthropology – that enables us to reach out to others and appreciate their potential and spiritual thirst. We echo St Ignatius' own prayer:

> Take, O Lord, and receive my entire liberty, my memory, my understanding and my whole will. All that I am and all that I possess You have given me: I surrender it all to You to be disposed of according to Your will. Give me only Your love and Your grace; with these I will be rich enough.[17]

. . . .

Questions for reflection

1   How easy is it for you to get in touch with your feelings? How do you discern what God might be saying through them?

2   When was the last time you wept? What might trigger the gift of tears in you?

3   These days, we are sensitive to the difference between appropriate touch, which is gentle, respectful, honouring, ministering, reverent; and inappropriate touch, which is invasive, exploitative, abusive. When do you think the use of touch is appropriate in the practice of prayer? How do you feel about praying with your fingertips?

4   How do you handle anger or frustration? What do you learn from the fourth gospel about this?

Prayer exercises

Praying with your fingertips

Go out into creation to put your fingers in what the Franciscan Bonaventure called 'the fingerprints of God'. Appreciate delicate petal, supple wood, weathered stone with its lichens, unyielding rock of pavement, sharp edge of flints. Stroke your palm across leaves, fondle the protruding veins of a leaf, the fragile bud full of promise. Rub your fingers against all kinds of bark: knotted, knobbled wood of trees and the fresh, supple wood of saplings. Caress God in the velvety leaf, in the silky surface of herbs. Brush your fingertips against gritty rough-hewn stone or over a polished smooth surface. Pick up items that you can hold gently in the palms of your hands. If possible, walk barefoot on wet grass. Feel the moist earth, the springy turf beneath your feet. Linger in God's creation.

Praying with a stone

Take a stone and hold it in the palm of your hand. Take a close look at it and admire its uniqueness. Are there rough and smooth parts to it? There is only one just like this, with its particular markings and structure. Make friends with it!

Its past: wonder to yourself – where has this stone come from? What is its past, its history? What great cliff or mountain was it once a part of? What is its geological story? Wonder about what happened to this rock. Was it pounded by the waves of the sea? Was it polished by the movement of ice?

Its future: what will become of this stone? Will it be taken by a youth and thrown through a window? Or just lie unwanted on the ground? Will this stone be used by a craftsman in a structure, a wall, an art installation? Will it be reshaped and remoulded carefully by an artist or a mason?

Finally, let this stone speak to you of your own life, past and future. You have a unique history and your own special gifting. Give thanks to God for his providence and provision. Thank God for your own 'markings' – those things about yourself, your appearance and personality that make you different.

How would you describe the present texture of your soul? Does it feel vulnerable, flaky, malleable, crumbly? Are there sharp edges? Any brittle or fragile parts? Are there parts that feel cracked or scarred, weathered, hardened or flaky? Does your soul feel in any way gravelly or gritty? Is it veined or streaked by recurring themes? What do you feel about any possible woundedness, vulnerabilities, cracks or fractures? Where are your strengths?

What parts of you might be named as resistances to God's formative purposes? Are you experiencing any friction in relation to God? What can you do to be more responsive to the purposes of God – whether that is akin to his work of erosion and wearing down, or to that of reshaping and building up?

As you hold the stone in your hands, realise that God holds you lovingly in his hands. He has plans for you. He desires to shape you and reshape your life – to mould you into his image, to accomplish his work of formation in you, to use you in the great building work of his kingdom. 'Like living stones, let yourselves be built into a spiritual house' (2 Peter 2:5). Rejoice that your life is raw material in the hands of the creator and redeemer God. Give thanks that he has an unfolding design and purpose for your unique life. Entrust yourself afresh to God, remembering: 'We are God's work of art' (Ephesians 2:9, NJB).

Praying with your hands

Use your hands expressively in this prayer time in four actions. Begin by clenching your fists tight and holding them before you. Feel the tension and let these fists represent an anger or frustration that bothers you today, or a situation in the world that you feel strongly about. Hold them before God in the solidarity of prayer and intercession.

Second, slowly open your downturned palms and let go of the tension. Let it fall away from you to God. In this gesture, give to God any negative feelings or stresses; feel them drip out of your fingertips, as it were. Surrender the situation to God's providence and sovereignty.

Third, turn your hands upwards in a gesture of surrender to God and of receiving from God. Breathe in what God wants to give you right now – perhaps a reassurance that all will be well. Breathe in his empowering Spirit, who will give you the courage for action.

Finally, take a look at your hands. Feel the creases, their complexion; trace the lines. They witness to your unique human journey, with its mix of pleasure and pain. But now they are ready to reach out to others, to touch others. Is there an action that God is calling you to make in relation to your initial concern? What should you do as a result of this – something bold, something risky or rebellious?

Praying with a hazelnut

Following the example of Julian of Norwich (c. 1342–1413), hold in the palm of your hand a flower, shell or something from creation – even a hazelnut. Using the eyes of your understanding, reflect on its beauty and on its fragility. Let it speak to you of your life, precious in God's hands. Read the extract below from Julian. Conclude with Psalm 139 and give thanks.

> Our good Lord showed me a spiritual sight of his familiar love. I saw that he is to us everything which is good and comforting for our help. He is our clothing, who wraps and enfolds us for love, embraces us and shelters us, surrounds us for his love, which is so tender that he may never desert us. And so in this sight I saw that he is everything which is good, as I understand.

And in this he showed me something small, no bigger than a hazelnut, lying in the palm of my hand, as it seemed to me, and it was as round as a ball. I looked at it with the eyes of my understanding and thought: What can this be? I was amazed that it could last, for I thought that because of its littleness it would suddenly have fallen into nothing. And I was answered in my understanding: It lasts and always will, because God loves it; and thus everything has being through the love of God.

In this little thing I saw three properties. The first is that God made it, the second is that God loves it, the third is that God preserves it. But what did I see in it? It is that God is the Creator and the protector and the lover. For until I am substantially united with him, I can never have perfect rest or true happiness, until, that is, I am so attached to him that there can be no created thing between my God and me.[18]

Praying with your breath

You can pray inhaling and exhaling with your breath in silence or using the Jesus Prayer or other mantra.

Breathe in, praying: 'Lord Jesus Christ, Son of God.'

Breathe out, praying: 'Have mercy on me, a sinner.'

This can be a way in which you are receiving Jesus and expelling sin. An alternative is praying for the fruits of the Spirit as your lungs fill with fresh air, saying,

'Hate' (out); 'love' (in). 'Fear' (out); 'trust' (in). 'Stress' (out); 'peace' (in). 'Worry' (out); 'joy' (in) – and so on using the passage in Galatians 5:19–24.

6

Glimpsing glory

In the awesome passage from Isaiah 6, where the prophet encounters the visible glory of God in the temple and offers himself in the words 'Here I am; send me!', he is immediately given some very perplexing words:

> Go and say to this people:
> 'Keep listening, but do not comprehend;
> keep looking, but do not understand.'
> Make the mind of this people dull,
>   and stop their ears, and shut their eyes,
> so that they may not look with their eyes,
>   and listen with their ears,
> and comprehend with their minds,
>   and turn and be healed.
> ISAIAH 6:9–10

This paradoxical text was obviously important for the first Christians; it is quoted in Matthew 13:14–15, Mark 8:18 and Acts 28:26–27. John uses it as a commentary on the poor rate of responsiveness among the people:

> He has blinded their eyes and hardened their heart, so that they might not look with their eyes, and understand with their heart and turn – and I would heal them.
> JOHN 12:40

Throughout the fourth gospel, Jesus is pained by those who see only superficially, who do not recognise the 'signs' in his 'works'. And he rejoices when people see deeply, discern the significance, and glimpse the Father in him: 'Whoever sees me sees him who sent me' (John 12:45).

'Come and see'

Throughout the fourth gospel, Jesus is seeking eyes wide open. He begins his ministry with the summons, the invitation: 'Come and see' (1:39). He himself is looking acutely: he turns and sees Andrew and Simon following him (1:38) and, looking intently at Simon (1:42), he gives him a new name and a new destiny. Next, he not only notices Nathaniel sitting under the fig tree, he also perceives the condition of his heart (1:47). As Nathaniel is stunned that Jesus should have such a penetrating gaze, Jesus responds: 'Do you believe because I told you that I saw you under the fig tree? You will see greater things than these... Very truly, I tell you, you will see heaven opened and the angels of God ascending and descending upon the Son of Man' (1:50–51). Jesus is offering, on earth, the very vision of heaven!

The invitation 'Come and see', first issued by Jesus, is taken up and echoed by Philip (1:46) and by the woman of Samaria (4:29). 'Come and look!' From the beginning to the end of the gospel, we are summoned to look, to open our eyes wide. The imperative 'Behold!' – 'Take a long look!' – is found from the Baptist to Pilate.

John the Baptist cries out: 'Look, here is the Lamb of God!' (1:36). On Palm Sunday, the evangelist quotes Zechariah: 'Look, your king is coming' (12:15). Even Pilate will say: 'Behold the man... behold your King!' (19:5, 14, KJV). We are directed to notice, peer beneath the surface, watch, contemplate, gaze, feast our eyes on the unfolding revelation. As John says in the prologue: 'No one has ever seen God. It is God the only Son, who is close to the Father's heart, who has made him known' (1:18).

The challenge, then, of this gospel is to open wide our eyes, minds and hearts. Jesus models this. In Galilee, he lifts up his eyes and sees a tide of human need approaching: a crowd – and he realises that they are doubly hungry: for food for their stomachs and for the bread of life for their souls (6:5). It is all about looking. 'And the Word became flesh and lived among us, and we have seen his glory, the glory as of a father's only son, full of grace and truth' (1:14). Jesus calls us to be curious, inquisitive, enquiring – not only to look, but also to see. He plays with this theme in chapter 4, where Jesus will say, emphatically: 'I tell you, lift up your eyes' (4:35, RSV).

Jesus looks in two directions

After the last supper, the evangelist tells us: 'After Jesus had spoken these words, he looked up to heaven and said, "Father, the hour has come"' (17:1). Jesus was *always* looking up to heaven, for 'the Son can do nothing on his own, but only what he sees the Father doing; for whatever the Father does, the Son does likewise' (5:19). Jesus lived in this world, with his eyes alert to human need and to the delights of creation, and at precisely the same time he is looking to heaven to glimpse his next move, to perceive what the Father is doing and directing: 'I declare what I have seen in the Father's presence' (8:38). The fourth gospel summons us to this double looking. We will focus on three passages, in chapters 9, 4 and 11.

True sight (John 9)

For John, the key to responding to Jesus lies in the looking. This theme is developed in the narrative of the healing of the man born blind in John 9. The account begins with Jesus opening his own eyes to human need. Jesus notices. 'As he walked along, he saw a man blind from birth' (9:1). It was possible for Jesus to pass by without comment as he made his way through the crowded streets of Jerusalem, but the evangelist tells us that, amidst the hustle and bustle of the city, Jesus observes. He spots the human need.

He goes on to respond with an unusual way of healing, which we considered in chapter 3. The man returns from the Pool of Siloam with eyes that see. Not only is he bombarded by all the sense impressions of the city, its sights and smells, but he is also beginning to recognise as well as see, to perceive the truth about Jesus. This is a gradual enlightenment. His main testimony is: 'Though I was blind, now I see' (9:25). Yet he realises that Jesus is, at least, a prophet (9:17). He goes on to make an astonishing affirmation: 'Never since the world began has it been heard that anyone opened the eyes of a person born blind. If this man were not from God, he could do nothing' (9:32–33).

Yet, in a story told with great humour by John, there is a creeping blindness obliterating the spiritual sight of the Pharisees:

> Some of the Pharisees near him heard this and said to him, 'Surely, we are not blind, are we?' Jesus said to them, 'If you were blind, you would not have sin. But now that you say, "We see", your sin remains.'
> JOHN 9:40–41

The Pharisees, who believed they possessed great insight into the Torah and understood the revelation from God, turn out to be self-blinded. Yet a man whom people passed without noticing turns out to have not only fresh eyes to see physically but inner perception to glimpse the truth about Jesus.

Looking differently: at water, food, fields (John 4)

While in Samaria, Jesus encounters a fixation with physical things and leads his hearers into a radically different way of looking at the world. Twice over, the woman at the well is stuck on a literal and physical hearing of Jesus' words: 'Sir, you have no bucket, and the well is deep. Where do you get that living water?... Sir, give me this water, so that I may never be thirsty or have to keep coming here to draw water' (4:11, 15). But Jesus wants to lead her from the physicality of the water to its sacramentality, and how it powerfully symbolises the gift of God. The physical water and the well speak to Jesus of humanity's deep thirst for things of the Spirit and God's gracious provision.

The disciples too are utterly bewitched by a concern for physical things. They had gone into the town to buy food (4:8). Upon their return, they urge him: 'Rabbi, eat something' (4:31). 'But he said to them, "I have food to eat that you do not know about." So the disciples said to one another, "Surely no one has brought him something to eat?"' (4:32–33).

Jesus sees food as highly symbolic and sacramental. In chapter 6, John will put on the lips of Jesus: 'The bread that I will give for the life of the world is my flesh' (6:51). There, he will be misunderstood and accused of advocating cannibalism. Another response will be to ask for a continual supply of free, fresh bread (6:34). His hearers stay on the level of the physical and cannot glimpse sacramentality. In Samaria, he explains: 'My food is to do the will of him who sent me' (4:34). He is not talking about a picnic brought to him. He is talking of the deep nourishment and sustenance that come from moving within the Father's will.

Jesus wants to open the disciples to a new vision and a fresh way of seeing reality. He calls them to become wide awake to the possibilities God is opening up: 'Look around you, and see how the fields are ripe for harvesting' (4:35). But he is not talking about Samaritan agriculture. The fields around them speak to Jesus of the growth of the kingdom and the spiritual harvest that has become imminent.

Seeing sacramentally
This sacramental way of viewing reality is a dominant theme in the fourth gospel. Jesus sees wine, vines, water, bread, sunlight and candlelight, even shepherding, as speaking of himself. Jesus looks at a seed and sees its potential if it perishes: 'Unless a grain of wheat

falls into the earth and dies, it remains just a single grain; but if it dies, it bears much fruit' (12:24). He glimpses his very destiny in a kernel of wheat.

The other gospels combine to give us the clear impression that this was an outlook on the world that was truly characteristic of Jesus himself. The secrets of the kingdom reveal themselves through parables of seed, mountain, field and sea (Matthew 13; Mark 11:23). Jesus says: 'Consider the lilies, how they grow' (Luke 12:27). 'Consider': the Greek word means 'turn your attention to this, notice what is happening, take note'. It is a summons to a contemplative way of life, a deeply reflective way of seeing the world. It stands in utter contrast with the way the woman and the disciples see things – they can't see past a bucket of water or a plate of food! 'Take a look around you,' Jesus says to the disciples. Learn to see things differently.

Glimpsing glory (John 11)

In the fourth gospel, we are not invited to see the 'works' of Jesus as miracles, as a sort of magic by a superhero or wonder-worker. Rather, we are invited to see them as 'signs' – clues, indicators of God's glory and presence.

John also invites us to see problems and even fatal illnesses as situations that are pregnant with the glory of God. John 11 begins with Martha sending an urgent request to Jesus: 'Lord, he whom you love is ill.' She hopes that Jesus will leave whatever he is doing, and come and heal her brother immediately. Martha is focusing on the presenting problem; she sees only illness, a brother who is sick. She acknowledges Jesus to be 'Lord' but seems closed in her thinking about what might happen. She expects, demands a miracle of healing. She wants Jesus on her own terms. She wants him as a problem-solver, who can come in with his magic and mend the situation. But he is very emphatic in his response to Martha's plea: 'This illness does not lead to death; rather it is for God's glory, so that the Son of God may be glorified through it' (11:4). Again, outside

Lazarus' tomb Jesus says to Martha: 'Did I not tell you that if you believed, you would see the glory of God?' (11:40).

Martha is invited to pray not for Lazarus' healing, but for the revelation of the glory of God. Do we, like her, have in fact too low an expectation of intercession, asking for restoration of a deteriorating situation when we could be asking for the revelation of the glory of God? Martha asked for Lazarus' healing from illness. What she goes on to receive is the astounding vision of Christ as the vanquisher of death, as Lazarus rises from the tomb. Moreover, she receives the salvation of the world for, in John's view, Lazarus' rising precipitates and leads directly to the crucifixion. To pray for a glimpse of glory is to open ourselves utterly to God, and to rule nothing out!

The evangelist is inviting us to turn our narrow-minded prayers of intercession ('Please help') into daring, risky cries like 'Lord, come and reveal your glory!' Martha has to let go of her small and narrow expectations and allow Christ to surprise her with the revelation of his glory, which is beyond her wildest imagination. As the letter to the Ephesians puts it:

> Now to him who by the power at work within us is able to accomplish abundantly far more than all that we ask or imagine, to him be glory in the church and in Christ Jesus to all generations, forever and ever. Amen
> EPHESIANS 3:20–21

Like Martha, we need to learn to give up any well-meaning tiny-mindedness. We must not confine God or box him into our inherited and preconceived ideas. We need to be open to the glory of Christ, however and whenever it is to be revealed, most likely in the places and people we would least expect to find it. We need too to make a transition from prescriptive, manipulative styles of intercession, which almost amount to a desire to control God – 'Lord, he whom you love is ill' or 'Meet this need' – to risky, open kinds of petition: 'Lord, come and reveal your glory!' We need to remember that intercession is inseparable from self-offering: as we bring a situation to God we bring ourselves and place ourselves, once again, at God's disposal.[1]

The cross: behold glory

All this climaxes at the cross. Greek pilgrims to Jerusalem declare: 'We wish to see Jesus' (12:21). He directs them to where they will most clearly see him: 'And I, when I am lifted up from the earth, will draw all people to myself' (12:32). The cross will be not so much an oblation as a revelation: crucifixion becomes glorification, abasement an enthronement. We will be invited to see in blood and water dripping from the pierced body of Christ the very birth of the church (represented in the mother and the beloved disciple embracing at the foot of the cross) and a sign of the sacraments (19:35; compare 1 John 5:6–8). Jesus' prayer is this:

> Father, I desire that those also, whom you have given me, may be with me where I am, to see my glory, which you have given me because you loved me before the foundation of the world.
> JOHN 17:24

The glory of God is supremely and paradoxically to be revealed on the cross. While other parts of the New Testament suggest that Jesus first suffers and then receives glory in the resurrection/ascension (Luke 24:26; Hebrews 2:9), John alone sees the crucifixion of Christ as the greatest moment of glorification. In the fourth gospel, Christ can say of his Passion: 'The hour has come for the Son of man to be glorified' (12:23; see also 7:39; 13:31; 17:1–5). Jesus approaches his death not as a disaster to be endured, but as a glory to be embraced, for the cross is the moment of salvation. From the cross flow forgiveness and hope – it is the greatest hour of God's revelation, the laying bare of his presence. Once again, it is all a matter of looking, of seeing in depth. John quotes the scripture (Zechariah 12:10): 'They will look on the one whom they have pierced.'

Easter Day

In his accounts of Easter, John's thoughts on the significance of looking reach their culmination. Peter and the beloved disciple race to the tomb: Peter sees the discarded graveclothes and makes no response, but the beloved disciple both 'saw and believed' – he recognises the sign, the evidence of the resurrection (20:1–10). When it comes to Thomas, he declares that if he does not see the wounds of Christ in his risen body with his own eyes, he cannot believe. Jesus will say: 'Have you believed because you have seen me? Blessed are those who have not seen and yet have come to believe' (20:29). Seeing is believing? We can believe the resurrection without physically setting eyes on the figure of the risen Lord. Yet we are invited to open our eyes wide and to glimpse the signs, the clues all around us. This is the testimony of Mary Magdalene and also of the disciples: 'We have seen the Lord!' (20:18, 25). Indeed, John's very claim to be able to write his gospel is that he is an eyewitness: 'He who saw this has testified so that you also may believe' (19:35).

. . . .

Spirituality of seeing

In his wonderful account of the risen Christ meeting the disciples on the road to Emmaus, Luke repeatedly uses the metaphor of spiritual sight:

> But their eyes were kept from recognising him… They stood still, looking sad… 'Some of those who were with us went to the tomb and found it just as the women had said; but they did not see him'… Then their eyes were opened, and they recognised him; and he vanished from their sight.
> LUKE 24:16–17, 24, 31

In the physicality of breaking bread together, they come to spiritual insight. Prayer enables an awakening of the spirit and the body: a coming fully alive, aware of and responsive to what God wanted to offer us. In prayer, we seek fresh vision, wider perspective. Of course, we can also be blinkered and suffer from spiritual myopia. Ephrem (d. 373), the prolific and inspiring Syriac writer, encourages us in prayer to see reality differently, using his famed image of the 'luminous eye', which can look into the hiddenness of God's mystery:

> Blessed is the person who has acquired a luminous eye
> With which he will see how much the angels stand in awe of You, Lord,
> And how audacious is man.[2]

Ephrem encourages us to pray for the gift of the inner eye, which penetrates the deep things of God and gives true insight. In this way, our prayer can become luminous, radiant and light-revealing:

> Let our prayer be a mirror, Lord, placed before Your face;
> Then Your fair beauty will be imprinted on its luminous surface.[3]

The third eye

Christian philosophers in 12th-century Paris, at the monastery of St Victor, open our eyes to new ways of seeing, fresh approaches to perception. First, Hugh of St Victor (1096–1141), distinguished between *cogitatio*, *meditatio*, and *contemplatio*. *Cogitatio*, or simple empirical cognition, is a seeking for the facts of the material world using the eye of flesh. *Meditatio* is a seeking for the truths within oneself (the *imago* of God) using the mind's eye. *Contemplatio* is the knowledge gained by transcendent insight, revealed by the eye of contemplation. Richard of St Victor (1110–73), building on this, affirmed that each level of sight and insight, represented in the three eyes, builds on the previous one.[4] We begin with utilising the first eye, the eye of flesh, through the senses. We progress by employing a second eye through meditation or reflection. But deepest vision is attained by the third eye – the inner eye – giving us glimpses of true understanding through contemplation. Rohr explains:

> Third-eye seeing is the way mystics see. They do not reject the first eye; the senses matter to them. Nor do they reject the second eye; but they know not to confuse knowledge with depth or mere correct information with the transformation of consciousness itself. The mystical gaze builds upon the first two eyes – and yet goes further. It happens whenever, by some wondrous 'coincidence', our heart space, our mind space and our body awareness are all simultaneously open and non-resistant... I like to call it *presence*. It is experienced as a moment of deep inner connection, and it always pulls you, intensely satisfied, into the naked and undefended now, which can include both profound joy and profound sadness at the same time. At that point, you either want to write poetry, pray or be utterly silent.[5]

In the next century, Eckhart (1260–1328) calls us to a high state of wakefulness, watchfulness and mindfulness, if we are to see God in this life:

> In all his acts and in all things a person should consciously use his reason, having in all things a perceptive awareness of himself and his inward being, and in all things seize God... For indeed, people who are expectant like that are watchful, they look around them to see where he whom they expect is coming from... This requires much diligence, demanding a total effort of our senses and powers of mind.[6]

Catherine of Siena summons us: 'Look into the depth... of divine charity. For unless you see you cannot love. The more you see, the more you can love.'[7]

St Francis de Sales called contemplation 'a loving, simple and permanent attentiveness of the mind to divine things'.[8] The

Catechism of the Catholic Church calls it 'a gaze of faith' and 'a silent love'.[9] A story from the Curé of Ars, St Jean-Marie-Baptiste Vianney, a 19th-century French priest, illustrates this memorably. He noticed a peasant come into church and stay for hours in front of the tabernacle, where the sacrament was reserved for the communion of the sick. The priest asked him: 'What do you say during all that time before Jesus in the Eucharist?' The farmer replied: 'Nothing! I look at him and he looks at me.'[10]

Seeking a bigger vision: the Cosmic Christ

Pierre Teilhard de Chardin (1881–1955), scientist and Jesuit, became captivated by an all-encompassing vision of the Cosmic Christ, existing in all things and sustaining all things. As he looked at the material world, his vision, his seeing, was inspired by this text:

> He is the image of the invisible God, the firstborn of all creation; for in him all things in heaven and on earth were created, things visible and invisible, whether thrones or dominions or rulers or powers – all things have been created through him and for him. He himself is before all things, and in him all things hold together.
>
> COLOSSIANS 1:15–17

He came to see Christ present in all things and as the fundamental principle of unity in a fragmenting world. He saw the Eucharist pointing to this truth:

> Grant, Lord, that your descent into the universal Species [of bread and wine] may not be for me just something loved and cherished, like the fruit of some philosophical speculation, but may become for me truly a real Presence. Whether we like it or not by power and by right you are incarnate in the world, and we are all of us dependent upon you... I firmly believe that everything around me is the body and blood of the Word.[11]

Inspired by Paul's vision 'that God may be all in all' (1 Corinthians 15:28), he believed that the world was in a state of continuous evolution understood as the divinisation of the universe. He prayed 'that in every creature I may discover and sense you, I beg you: give me faith'.[12] In another place, he writes:

> A tremendous spiritual power is slumbering in the depth of our multitude, which will manifest itself only when we have learnt to break down the barriers of our egoisms and, by a fundamental recasting of our outlook, raise ourselves up to the habitual and practical vision of universal realities.[13]

Fresh visions

Prayer invites us to catch a glimpse of the bigger picture, the wider vision, the broader vista, which will give renewed meaning and purpose to our lives. We conclude with a look at a recent writer, who finds in spirituality clues to a greater vision, moving from Jesus of Nazareth to the Cosmic Christ. Franciscan Ilia Delio, standing as a scientist and Christian within the tradition of de Chardin, ends her recent work *Christ in Evolution* like this:

> We must liberate Christ from a western intellectual form that is logical, abstract, privatised and individualised... Christ is the power of God among us and within us, the fullness of the earth and of life in the universe... We can look forward toward that time when there will be one cosmic person uniting all persons, one cosmic humanity uniting all humanity, one Christ in whom God will be all in all.[14]

How big is your vision? Is your God too small? Johann Baptist Metz puts it:

> Christian witnessing to God is guided through and through by political spirituality, a political mysticism. Not a mysticism of political power and political domination, but rather – to speak

metaphorically – a mysticism of open or opened eyes. Not only the ears for hearing, but also the eyes are organs of grace!… In the end Jesus did not teach an ascending mysticism of closed eyes, but rather a God-mysticism with an increased readiness for perceiving, a mysticism of open eyes, which sees more and not less.[15]

. . . .

Questions for reflection

1 How can your prayer become more mystical and, at the same time, more in touch with the world? What is your experience of prayer as a space and process enabling the shifting and enlarging of perceptions?

2 'I had heard of you by the hearing of the ear, but now my eye sees you' (Job 42:5). What is your experience of 'the three eyes?'

3 What do you make of Richard Rohr's affirmation (in *Dancing Standing Still*), 'This should be the early form of spiritual teaching: not what to see, but how to see'?[16]

4 What are you learning from John's gospel about the art of seeing?

5 How is it possible to retrain ourselves to see the world sacramentally: discovering God in the details, as well as in 'the bigger picture'? What do you think might be signs of myopia? What would help?

Prayer exercise

Either
Take another walk in your neighbourhood with the character of intentionality (deliberate purpose) to watch and look with alertness. Be prepared to be surprised, delighted and disturbed by God in what you encounter.

Afterwards, reflect: it was not a matter of taking God to the community, but rather of discovering God right there. He got there before you, of course! Where is he lurking? What are you noticing? Celebrate 'God in all things'.

Or
In a group or alone, bring to a table set before you, as a visual focus, objects or symbols that speak to you somehow of God. Place them reverently before you and feast your eyes on them. How do you glimpse the divine in them? If in a group, share perceptions. Conclude with George Herbert's 1633 hymn:

> *Teach me, my God and King,*
> *   In all things Thee to see,*
> *And what I do in anything*
> *   To do it as for Thee…*
>
> *A man that looks on glass,*
> *   On it may stay his eye;*
> *Or if he pleaseth, through it pass,*
> *   And then the heaven espy.*
>
> *All may of Thee partake;*
> *   Nothing can be so mean,*
> *Which with this tincture – 'for Thy sake' –*
> *   will not grow bright and clean.*

A servant with this clause
Makes drudgery divine:
Who sweeps a room, as for Thy laws,
Makes that and the action fine.

This is the famous stone
That turneth all to gold;
For that which God doth touch and own
Cannot for less be told.

7

Hearing God's voice

The word 'hear' occurs 56 times in the fourth gospel. Many sounds are evoked. At the beginning of the narrative, we hear the bleating of frightened animals driven out from the temple, the clatter of overturned tables and the cries of the protesting traders. We catch an echo of the sobbing of a woman taken in adultery and the howling of her accusers; the whining of mourners at the tomb of Lazarus. There are liquid sounds: the thrashing of waves in the storm on the lake; the gurgling of water carefully poured into stone jars 'up to the brim'; the sploshing of the blind man coming to sight in the waters of Siloam; the dribbling and splashing of water over dirty feet. In the Passion, we can almost hear the swish of Pilate's lashing, scourging whip slicing the air, and the fizz and crackle of charcoal fires burning in the high priest's courtyard, and later on the lakeshore. We hear the sound of the sign being hammered into the top of the wooden cross, and the tearing and ripping apart of Jesus' garments. We listen to Mary Magdalene's breathlessness as she runs to the tomb, and the raucous, anxious race of Peter and the beloved disciple to the site. We almost hear the sound of the door to the upper room being bolted and locked 'for fear'. Finally, we hear cries of excitement and disbelief as Peter springs into Galilee's waters to reach out to Jesus.

Sometimes, the text deliberately alerts us to the physicality of sound – we are prompted to hear the whoosh and whistle of the wind in our ears, encountering the energy and mystery of God's breath: 'The wind blows where it chooses, and you hear the sound of it' (3:8). When, at the visit of the Greeks to Jerusalem, the Father speaks from heaven, John narrates: 'The crowd standing there heard it and said that it was thunder' (12:29). But this was not the crashing together of clouds, rumbling and reverberating in surprised ears, but a declaration from heaven: 'Jesus answered, "This voice has come for your sake, not for mine"' (12:30). So listening has a special theological significance for the gospel of John. What matters most is that we listen to God: 'In the beginning was the Word.' From the deep silences of eternity, the Word goes forth: it is enfleshed, and it becomes audible. The Word finds a body and a voice.

Jesus models listening to the Father

Before the Word speaks, he listens. The Jesus of John's gospel can only share and reveal what he himself has heard from his Father: 'He testifies to what he has seen and heard, yet no one accepts his testimony' (3:32). Jesus is emphatic: 'The one who sent me is true, and I declare to the world what I have heard from him' (8:26). He describes himself as 'a man who has told you the truth that I heard from God' (8:40). He is clear: 'The word that you hear is not mine, but is from the Father who sent me' (14:24). The fourth gospel is offered to us by the beloved disciple, giving the impression that he was not only there with Jesus but even eavesdropping on his conversation with his Father.

Just as the beloved disciple had himself lain on the breast of Jesus, so 'it is God the only Son, who is close to the Father's heart [lit. 'bosom'], who has made him known' (1:18). Jesus declares: 'I can do nothing on my own. As I hear, I judge' (5:30).

Jesus models listening to others

Jesus reveals a close listening to the other in John's gospel. He hears the cries of the hungry (John 6). Jesus hears about the needs of the moment as he listens to his mother at Cana's wedding (John 2). He listens attentively to the paralytic's story (John 5). He hears the sobs of Mary Magdalene and asks: 'Why are you weeping?' (20:15). We notice that, in his listening, Jesus does not hold back from asking open questions that will aid his knowledge and understanding of the situation.

We must listen

The gospel narrative starts with listening. 'The two disciples heard him say this, and they followed Jesus' (1:37). They catch the echo of his words and the import of his words.

Later, the Samaritans testify to the woman at the well: 'It is no longer because of what you said that we believe, for we have heard for ourselves, and we know that this is truly the Saviour of the world' (4:42). They had heard first-hand, and the listening experience for them was transformational: they would never be the same again.

To Pilate, Jesus says: 'Everyone who belongs to the truth listens to my voice' (18:37).

The voice calls us to adventure

This is a key theme in chapter 10:

> The gatekeeper opens the gate for him, and the sheep hear his voice. He calls his own sheep by name and leads them out... I have other sheep that do not belong to this fold. I must bring them also, and they will listen to my voice. So there will be one flock, one shepherd... My sheep hear my voice. I know them, and they follow me.
> JOHN 10:3, 16, 27

Jesus offers himself to the world as a shepherd. He wishes to go before us: 'He calls his own sheep by name and leads them *out*' (10:3) – that is, out of the comfort zone, out from the security and safety of the sheepfold's enclosure, and into the risky and potentially dangerous open fields of the countryside. We are given the image of Jesus as shepherd, striding across the hills: 'When he has brought out all his own, he goes ahead of them, and the sheep follow him because they know his voice' (10:4).

We note three challenges:

- We need to attune ourselves to somehow actually hear the call of Christ.
- We have to listen amidst the cacophony of competing demands. Clamouring voices compete for our attention: 'All who came before me are thieves and bandits; but the sheep did not listen to them' (10:8).
- If we listen to Jesus, we must be ready for an adventurous journey, because he leads us *out*.

The voice calls us to life

The voice of Jesus wakes the dead! The teaching of chapter 5 anticipates the events of chapter 11:

> Very truly, I tell you, anyone who hears my word and believes him who sent me has eternal life, and does not come under judgement, but has passed from death to life. Very truly, I tell you, the hour is coming, and is now here, when the dead will hear the voice of the Son of God, and those who hear will live... Do not be astonished at this; for the hour is coming when all who are in their graves will hear his voice.
> JOHN 5:24–25, 28

Jesus speaks these words as a defence of his healing at the Pool of Bethesda on the sabbath. There, the paralysed man, for 38 years a cripple and fixed to the spot by the water's edge, represents all in captivity and symbolises the dead. He hears the voice of Jesus, who begins by challenging his despondency and his depressed resignation: 'Do you want to be healed?' (5:6, RSV). The first thing that the man hears is a penetrating question, striking right at his heart. The second thing sounds like a call to resurrection: 'Rise, take up your pallet, and walk' (5:8, RSV). Jesus calls him from a living death to his greatest potential. Most significantly, Jesus encounters the man, now healed, in the one place from which he has been excluded all his life, owing to his deformity being unacceptable to the religious authorities: 'Jesus found him in the temple' (5:14). The man is restored to his fullest dignity in the sight of God. The voice of Jesus has truly called him from death to fullness of life.

In John 11, it is first the sisters Mary and Martha who must hear the voice of Jesus: 'The Teacher is here and is calling for you' (11:28). The words of Jesus shatter their illusions and explode their inherited ideas about how God should work. When Jesus arrives at the tomb of Lazarus, the theme of hearing is highlighted. First, Jesus is the one listening – to the Father: 'Jesus looked upward and said, "Father, I thank you for having heard me. I knew that you always hear me, but I have said this for the sake of the crowd standing here, so that they may believe that you sent me."' Second, Jesus calls out to the dead man: 'He cried with a loud voice: "Lazarus, come out!"' Jesus gives the order: 'Unbind him, and let him go' (11:41–44). But it is not only Lazarus who has been liberated by hearing the voice of Jesus. There is the unbinding and freeing of the sisters from their narrow views and inherited dogmas.

. . . .

Spirituality of listening

Listening to God

Teresa of Avila (1515–82) uses powerful and memorable images to encourage us to make a shift in moving from talkative prayer to the prayer of listening, a movement from pious chatter to stillness, and the discovery of 'the Prayer of Quiet'. She develops very creatively the patristic concept of the Triple Way, which suggests that the spiritual journey will go through three major phases of purgation/repentance, illumination/receptive prayer and union.[1] Teresa uses this as a basis for shaping the spiritual journey she describes in *The Interior Castle*. Depicting the soul as a crystal castle with many rooms, Christ dwelling at the centre, she invites the reader to trace a journey through successive stages in order to reach a state of mystical union. The image conveys the beauty and potential of the soul; the door to the castle, and indeed its weaving corridor, is the experience of prayer.

The adventure of prayer begins with 'the Purgative Way' of prayer in the first three rooms of the Teresa's interior castle. They represent an increasing detachment from the noisy clamour of the world and a process of deepening repentance and humility. In the first room of self-knowledge, Teresa's cries: 'O souls redeemed by the blood of Jesus Christ! Learn to understand yourselves!... The soul's capacity is much greater than we can realise.'[2] In the second room, Teresa calls the reader to have 'a very determined determination' – a deep resolve to conquer the pull to turn back to the attractions of the world, in order to remain very focused and single-minded in the interior journey. The third room describes the stability and predictability of respectable routines and normal disciplines of the Christian life, such as active, discursive meditation. This is the room that we normally get stuck in. Prayer is defined here as 'talking to God' and so is wordy, chatty, verbose and busy. But Teresa says, whatever room we may be in, let us notice that there is a door opposite, beckoning us to step into another room, and into a richer experience of God.

A sign or indicator that the soul is ready to move on from this third room reveals itself in a holy restlessness or discontent with unfulfilling dutiful praying – a craving for a greater interior freedom and a desire to jump off the treadmill of Christian life. This marks a turning point in the journey, and a readiness for transition into the next phase. It is time to learn new ways of praying.

The journey takes a major step forward into 'the Illuminative Way' through Teresa's fourth room: a place of new discovery which opens us up to 'supernatural prayer'. Humphreys explains:

> Supernatural prayer is where God takes over. It is also called infused contemplation, passive prayer, mystical prayer, or infused prayer. All labels, again, mean the same thing. This type of prayer means that God is communicating with the person.[3]

Teresa advises:

> If you would progress a long way on this road and ascend to the mansions of your desire, the important thing is not to think much, but to love much; do, then, whatever most arouses you to love.[4]

The heart becomes enlarged (Psalm 119:32): there is a greater capacity for prayer, a letting go of former restrictive practices of prayer and a movement from the primacy of ego to the initiative of God. We are discovering the prayer that listens.

Subversive silence

Contemporary society is filled with sound-making gadgetry. We have iPods, iPads, iPhones, iPlayers, smartphones, MP3 players, and so on. It seems people can't walk along the street without pumping some noise into their brains. We see people of all ages, walking even in the country with something stuck into their ears – headphones or earpieces, blaring out 'music', of sorts. Is this continual need to fill our heads with entertainment actually a strategy of avoidance, preventing us from being reflective or confronting the hard issues of life and death? It has become a way in which people protect themselves from facing the deeper issues. They are connected – to noise, music, networks – but weirdly disconnected from themselves. The stresses and strains mount up; they don't go away.

Silence subverts and unsettles conventional attitudes. There is something paradoxical about silence. It seems an emptiness but reveals a fullness; it seems an absence of something but affords the chance to sense and experience the palpable presence of God. Silence feels like something is missing, but in fact leads to finding something precious, making a great discovery. Silence brims with the presence of God.

Spending half an hour in silence seems like a waste of time but could turn out to be a big investment, if we get in touch with our deepest selves and in touch with God. It sounds like achieving nothing but through it we could be gaining a fresh perspective on things. Stillness reorients us and brings space into our chaotic, frenetic lives. Silence gives us a chance to catch up with ourselves and get in touch with our truest longings. Like the desert, so important in Christian spirituality, it allows no hiding place. It is a time to be real, real with God and real with ourselves too. Going into silence might look like escapism from the world but actually turns out to be a needful reality check. There is an immediacy about silence – in it, we are plunged into truth, confronted by ourselves and by God. Like the desert, silence can be inviting and threatening, affirming but maybe disturbing. Recently, clergy have been speaking to me about this.[5] One said: 'Silence gives oxygen to my soul.' Another put it this way: 'Silence sorts me out, but I don't understand how that happens.'

Why is it that we do almost anything to avoid silence? Is it its truth-telling quality? Silence can be a scary, intimidating place to be, because in it we come face-to-face, as it were, with God and our own reality. It confronts us with our own aloneness and mortality. But, strangely and beautifully, silence communicates the accepting love of God. It does not judge us or utter pronouncements; it simply holds us in being, just as we are. It enfolds us, embraces us, reassures us that all will be well. And it is strangely rejuvenating too, healing, even – perhaps because we are giving God a chance to work on us. Above all, the practice of silence creates a space where we can learn to listen, once again.

Listening to others

We discover how the practice of contemplative listening becomes a 'transferable skill', which prepares us and equips us to relate meaningfully to our contemporary culture. Meaningful interaction with others entails attentive listening to the other. Listening requires a focused attentiveness to the other.

A double listening is required before any speaking, any evangelism: a listening to God and a discovery of the hopes and hurts in our community. As the report *mission-shaped church* puts it: 'This process involves listening to the culture... and to the inherited tradition of the gospel and the church.'[6] We need to attune ourselves both to what God is saying in the historic riches of spirituality, for example, and also to what God is saying in the people of our society today.

First, we learn to listen inwardly:

- to our own heart, our feelings and responses to God
- to the inner word of God: his whispers and intimations
- to the word of God in scripture to us.

But we also learn to listen to what God is saying to us outwardly:

- the cries of the poor
- the screams of the oppressed
- the sobs of the broken-hearted
- the sighs of our culture
- the laughter in people's lives.

Today, we face noise pollution almost everywhere – not only the roar of traffic and the blast of music, but a cacophony of competing demands and voices clamouring for attention. It is difficult to discern the voice of God, but we need to learn to listen to what 'the Spirit is saying to the churches' and to read the 'signs of the times'. Richard Foster encourages us:

Meditate upon the events of our time and... seek to penetrate their significance. We have a spiritual obligation to penetrate the inner meaning of events and political pressures, not to gain power, but to gain prophetic perspective.[7]

As we engage with the practice of such discipline, we discover where people are hurting, and where human dignity is being eroded. We echo Isaiah's comment: 'The Lord God has opened my ear' (Isaiah 50:5). The scripture is emphatic: 'O that today you would listen to his voice!' (Psalm 95:7).

Sometimes, God speaks to us through unexpected means. C.S. Lewis put it powerfully:

God whispers to us in our pleasures, speaks to us in our conscience, but shouts to us in our pains: it is his megaphone to rouse a deaf world... No doubt pain as God's megaphone is a terrible instrument; it may lead to final and unrepented rebellion. But it gives the only opportunity the bad man can have for amendment. It removes the veil; it plants the flag of truth within the fortress of a rebel soul.[8]

Lewis suggests that the experience of pain can shatter the illusion that all is well with us, destroying the false idea that we can get by very nicely without God. Pain shatters the illusion of self-sufficiency, for it causes us to reach out to God in either petition or complaint. It makes us wake up to the big questions of God and evil, and can draw us into a new surrender to God, the communion for which we were created. Suffering does indeed have a revelatory character, for those with eyes to see it. God speaks most powerfully through the experience of poverty and pain, calling us to simplicity and trust.

Using the ears of your heart

In the Christian tradition, the call to listen is frequent. The *Rule* of St Benedict opens with the imperative 'Listen!' and then goes on: 'Listen with the ear of your heart.' This is a deep and contemplative sort of listening. As the *Book of Common Prayer*'s intercessions put it, may the congregation both 'hear and receive thy holy word'. It is a receptive, non-judgemental listening that we're called to – the sort that is able to suspend judgement and let go of imposing our own agendas and solutions. This is a listening that is utterly open – open to surprises and unshockable!

The Quaker Douglas Steere puts it: 'To listen another's soul into a condition of disclosure and discovery may be almost the greatest service that any human being ever performs for another.'[9] The listening that we must practise requires, then, a readiness to move, literally and metaphorically, towards the other. It requires our awareness and attention. It is intentionally focused on the other. It must remain open-ended in the sense that it is not directed towards an outcome. It builds trust and enables true dialogue in which we suspend personal opinion and judgement. We listen in order to discover what we might learn from worlds outside our own. We hone our skills in beginning to see things from another's perspective. In learning to listen with attentiveness to others, we start to listen to God.

• • • • • • • • • • • • • • • • • •

Questions for reflection

1   Why is it, do you think, that Christians often prefer talkative prayer to listening prayer?

2   What is your experience of what Teresa calls 'the Prayer of Quiet'? Do you find silence inviting or intimidating?

3   'I see the sights that dazzle, the tempting sounds I hear' (from 'O Jesus, I have promised' by John Ernest Bode, 1816–74). What sounds tempt you? Which sounds intrigue you? Which disturb you?

4   Where and how do you hear God?

5   How can you retune your spiritual antennae to hear the whisper of God in all things?

Prayer exercise

> Morning by morning he wakens –
>   wakens my ear
>   to listen as those who are taught.
> ISAIAH 50:4

Take a prayer walk, with the intention of listening acutely and keenly. What sounds do you notice? Attune yourself to the environment, natural or man-made. Practise attentiveness… to the hum of bees, the whisper of the breeze, the echo of the ricochet of voices, the rumble of traffic, the sound of your own footprints and the rustle of your clothes… What do you hear of God in all this? Linger and listen. Try to detect how your heart responds.

Conclude with Bonar's prayer based on John's gospel and the theme of listening:

I heard the voice of Jesus say,
'Come unto Me and rest;
Lay down, thou weary one, lay down
Thy head upon My breast.'
I came to Jesus as I was,
Weary and worn and sad;
I found in Him a resting place,
And He has made me glad.

I heard the voice of Jesus say,
'Behold, I freely give
The living water; thirsty one,
Stoop down, and drink, and live.'
I came to Jesus, and I drank
Of that life-giving stream;
My thirst was quenched, my soul revived,
And now I live in Him.

I heard the voice of Jesus say,
'I am this dark world's Light;
Look unto Me, thy morn shall rise,
And all thy day be bright.'
I looked to Jesus, and I found
In Him my Star, my Sun;
And in that light of life I'll walk
Till trav'ling days are done.

Horatius Bonar (1846)

8

Tasting eternity

[Wisdom] has prepared a great banquet,
    mixed the wines, and set the table.
She has sent her servants to invite everyone to come.
    She calls out from the heights overlooking the city.
'Come in with me,' she urges the simple...
'Come, eat my food,
    and drink the wine I have mixed.
Leave your simple ways behind, and begin to live.'
PROVERBS 9:2–6 (NLT)

The image of Wisdom lies behind the *Logos* in John's prologue as God's playmate in creating the world (Proverbs 8). In the next chapter of the gospel, Wisdom is setting a table and summoning the world to dine with her. In John's gospel, we are invited to 'taste and see that the Lord is good' (Psalm 34:8). The narrative of Jesus' ministry begins with a party, a wedding festival (John 2). It ends with a delicious meal by the water's edge in Galilee (John 21): 'Come and eat' (21:12, GNT) is the invitation of the risen Lord on the lake shore. The Passion narrative is prefaced by a meal at the home of Lazarus, Mary and Martha (John 12) and is dominated by the last supper shared with the disciples as the context for the most profound teaching of the gospel.

We encounter in the fourth gospel a Jesus who is literally thirsty and hungry. As a pilgrim and wayfarer on the road, he seeks refreshment: 'Jesus, tired out by his journey, was sitting by the well. It was about noon. A Samaritan woman came to draw water, and Jesus said to her, "Give me a drink"' (4:6–7). On the cross, Jesus cries out: 'I am thirsty' (19:28). The visit to Samaria finds Jesus to be hungry. But while his stomach may be rumbling, his deepest hunger, as we noted, is for the Father's will.

In this chapter, we explore how physicality once again points to spirituality in the fourth gospel, and how basic, primal sensations of hunger and thirst carry significant theological messages about life: the quenching and fulfilling of our deepest needs. We explore three aspects: wine to gladden our hearts, water to quench the soul and bread for the journey.

Wine to gladden our hearts

Three themes stand out in the joyous gathering set in Cana of Galilee.

Celebration

Jesus invites us to rejoice in God's gifts. Stunningly, the wedding at Cana reveals the exuberance of God's generosity. Whether we read it as history or parable, its message is unmistakable. We are awed by the sheer quantity of wine that John tells us Jesus produces: six stone water jars, each holding 20 or 30 gallons. Jesus turns 180 gallons of water into wine, the first of his signs, in John's view setting the tone and priority for his ministry. In our terms, that is 1,168 bottles of our normal 70cl size – or 194 boxes of wine. What a party for a small village! (Archaeology reveals that the population of nearby Nazareth was about 200 at the time of Christ, and Cana was a lot smaller.) This joyous extravagance testifies to a theme John introduces in his prologue: 'From his fullness we have all received, grace upon grace' (1:16). The luscious wine is described (2:10, NIV) as 'the best'!

Revelation

But all is not what it seems. We are invited to look beneath the surface and glimpse an epiphany taking place. This is no mere event, or happening, it is a *sign* – but a sign of what? What does it point to? John says: 'Jesus did this, the first of his signs, at Cana of Galilee, and revealed his glory' (2:11).

In John's perspective, the divine glory just beneath the surface is unleashed in the signs of Jesus. In these events, the glory breaks out visibly and tangibly. But they all point to the greatest epiphany: the wondrous theophany of the cross. At Cana's wedding, Christ tastes the best wine ever. But on the cross, his lips will receive a different drink, for the 'best wine' of Cana points forward to 'the sour wine' of Calvary:

> After this, when Jesus knew that all was now finished, he said (in order to fulfil the scripture), 'I am thirsty.' A jar full of sour wine was standing there. So they put a sponge full of the wine on a branch of hyssop and held it to his mouth. When Jesus had received the wine, he said, 'It is finished.' Then he bowed his head and gave up his spirit.
>
> JOHN 19:28–30

At Cana, Jesus says to Mary: 'My hour has not yet come' (2:4). Cana precipitates the dawning of the 'hour' of his Passion, and is followed by the event in the temple where the foes of Jesus already take their place in the unfolding drama. So John calls this a sign – it is symbolic; it is sacramental. What is its deeper message?

Transformation

John calls it 'the first of his signs' (2:11). The party at Cana is ultimately about God changing lives. *That* is why it is at the start of the gospel narrative, and sets Jesus' tone for what is to follow. The changing of water into wine symbolises Jesus' power to transform lives. He takes the stuff of ordinary life – water – and turns it into the new wine of the kingdom. Indeed, each of John's seven signs testifies to the transformation Christ brings, changing lives forever and healing the deepest needs of humanity.

Water to quench the soul

The two most significant references to water are found in chapter 4 and chapter 7. To the woman drawing supplies at Jacob's Well, Jesus says this:

> If you knew the gift of God… you would have asked him, and he would have given you living water… Those who drink of the water that I will give them will never be thirsty. The water that I will give will become in them a spring of water gushing up to eternal life.
>
> JOHN 4:10, 14

Jesus promises a Spirit who quenches our deepest thirst, an inner geyser, welling up to eternal life.

In John's perspective, Jesus takes his disciples to Samaria in order to expose them to radical paradigm shifts. Jesus leads the disciples from denial to embrace, in relation to the other. Notice how John frames the account in chapter 4. Immediately preceding it, he says: 'Now a discussion about purification arose between John's disciples and a Jew' (3:25). The issue of purification was a major preoccupation of the Jewish people at this time, and a special concern of the Pharisees. It was about two things: preserving identity in a pagan environment, and worthiness to approach God. Living under Roman occupation, with imperial values, deities and morals gaining increasing influence since Pompey's invasion in 67BC, the Jewish people had to attend closely to safeguarding their culture and identity. This had been an age-old concern, of course, but now it was an urgent issue once again: how can Jews live as a separate people, retaining their heritage and sense of distinctness, in the midst of occupation by a foreign power? Pharisees sought to preserve purity of *time* through observance of sabbath, Passover and festivals, and purity of *place* by having strict zones of demarcation around the temple, designating limits of access for the different groups of women and Gentile believers. They preserved purity of *body* by ritual washings and immersion pools (*mikveh*), by adhering to the rite of circumcision and by maintaining scrupulous rules about diet and food preparation. These were of central concern and often the subject of Jesus' critique (Luke 11:37–44; Mark 7:1–15; Matthew 23).[1]

The issue of purity was essentially about boundaries and barriers: who belongs or not; who are to be welcomed as insiders and who are to be rejected as outsiders. But it was not only a cultural concern but a religious concern, for only the purified, uncontaminated and orthodox were deemed fit to approach God in worship. So John notes this concern: 'a discussion about purification'. He follows it with Jesus striding into the most unpurified and defiling environment of Samaria, trailing his disciples in his wake!

Actions speak louder than words. Jesus chooses to sit down alongside a person who is triply suspect. First, the person is a woman. As John notes: '[The disciples] were astonished that he was speaking with a woman, but no one said, "What do you want?" or "Why are you speaking with her?"' (4:27). They were flabbergasted, but did not have the courage to challenge or even question Jesus. Second, she is a Samaritan, despised in Jewish eyes, a source of contamination. Third, she turns out to be a woman with some experience, having had five husbands and a present lover.

Jesus is crossing boundaries, defying conventions, smashing taboos. His promise to the woman of living water declares: you are worth it! You are acceptable to God! He wants to fill you with his Spirit![2] You may have a history – you may have wider experience than most – but God wants you! No wonder the disciples were astonished – confounded. Their minds have to make a somersault.

The living water promised to the woman is not for the purposes of washing, cleansing or purification. There is no suggestion here that she needs baptismal cleansing, though this had formerly been a concern in John 3 and at the start of chapter 4. Rather, Jesus is hailing her potential and her worthiness: 'The water that I will give will become in them a spring of water gushing up to eternal life' (4:14). When Jesus looks at this woman, he does not look in judgement or condemnation. He celebrates her capacity to bear the living water. He sees the possibilities within. Indeed, one who was an outcast and a reject becomes an evangelist and ambassador for the gospel. Jesus is unlocking the latent gifts in her. Soon, she will leave her still-empty water jar and rush back into the city saying: 'Come and see a man who told me everything I have ever done!' (4:29).

John is telling us that all people, of whatever ethnicity, orientation or gender, are worthy of becoming recipients of the living water. And to emphasise this point, he has the whole village declaring at the end of the story: 'We have heard for ourselves, and we know that this is truly the Saviour of the world!' (4:42). The Greek word for 'world' is, we noted, *cosmos*. Jesus is a cosmic phenomenon! He is opening to all people, of every background, an equal place in God's kingdom.

In this shift, this transition, Jesus asks us today to examine our own prejudices and short-sightedness. Where do they come from? What sustains prejudice? Does it have something to do with our own lack of a sense of security in God's love? Who is the Samaritan woman in your situation? Will you ever find her – dare you go to the well?

We imbibed Jesus' teaching on the water of the Spirit in chapter 3. Here, let's note how, in his glorious promise of the river of God (7:37–39), Jesus suggests three steps the disciples need to take: 'If anyone thirsts, let them come to me and drink. Out of their heart will flow rivers of living water.' They must first acknowledge and recognise their thirst for the Spirit. Second, they need to come to Jesus the giver of the Spirit and place themselves in expectant relation to him. Third, they are invited to drink and receive afresh the living water. In our prayer, we can take these three steps: we can thirst, come to Jesus and drink, receiving afresh the Spirit of God.

Bread for the journey

Reading the narrative of chapter 6, we are often quick, with John himself, to spiritualise the event of the feeding of the 5,000. But behind this story are actual pangs of hunger and painfully rumbling stomachs. Before we consider the awesome eucharistic references here, we need to get real about the actual situation of physical hunger.

The Galilee of Jesus' time suffered the double trouble of oppression and poverty. Lee writes: 'Galileans... were oppressed, dehumanised and looked down upon. Galileans were marginalised by foreign invaders and also by the Jerusalem temple-state.'[3] But, above all, it was a place of deep poverty and need. The Galileans were crippled by heavy taxes: dues were owed to the Roman occupier, and temple taxes added to the burden.

At the time of Jesus, ordinary families were being forced to quit their ancestral landholdings, where they had lived for centuries, in order to meet these demands. Land was also confiscated for the building projects and villas of the urban elite at Sepphoris and Tiberias. But then they had to pay rent for what had been their own fields and homes: they became caught in a downward economic spiral, becoming tenants in their own property. Tax and rent robbed the Galilean peasant farmer of two-thirds of the family income. Many were living at barely subsistence level,[4] while the Greco-Roman culture in Galilee nourished the creation of an upper class, the social elites, who owned great homes and estates. It was a world of 'haves' and 'have-nots'.

John's gospel tells us: 'Jesus realised that they were about to come and take him by force to make him king' (6:15). The people want Jesus to be a political messiah, bringing deliverance from the Roman occupiers. They want a king. But Jesus will not take this path, and decisively turns his back on this option. He is called to be not a political king, but bread to be shared for the world.

'Very truly, I tell you, you are looking for me, not because you saw signs, but because you ate your fill of the loaves' (6:26). But actual physical pangs of hunger do point to spiritual need, and the loaves point to eucharistic feeding. There remains a startling physicality to the words of Jesus that the first hearers find hard to accept: 'So Jesus said to them, "Very truly, I tell you, unless you eat the flesh of the Son of Man and drink his blood, you have no life in you"' (6:53). The hearers ask: 'How can this man give us his flesh to eat?' The Eucharist is not comfort food. There is a shocking dimension. The bread we eat at the altar must always remind us of both human hunger and the physicality of the incarnation, of the Word made flesh.

. . . .

Spirituality of food and drink

Feeding and ingesting: feasting on word and sacrament

Paul regularly resorts to the imagery of eating and feeding as he looks for metaphors of spiritual growth:

> And so, brothers and sisters, I could not speak to you as spiritual people, but rather as people of the flesh, as infants in Christ. I fed you with milk, not solid food, for you were not ready for solid food. Even now you are still not ready, for you are still of the flesh.
>
> 1 CORINTHIANS 3:1–3

Devour the word

The discipline of *lectio divina*, the slow, ponderous, meditative reading of scripture developed by Benedict and the monastic tradition, has been likened to 'slow eating'. There are four stages. First, *lectio* invites us to take a bite, to read a passage attentively, alert to particular words that strike us. Second, in *meditatio*, we can hold the word in our mind and heart as a piece of fruit might be held in the mouth: we take time to ask the Holy Spirit to lead us to its deepest meaning. Third, in *oratio*, we savour its taste, bitter or sweet or surprising, and allow this to lead us into a kind of prayer that dares ask questions of God: What are you saying? How might I have to change? In this phase, we expose to God's word our deepest needs and hopes. The word will heal, disturb, invigorate. Finally, in *contemplatio* we digest the word, welcome the word within our very selves, integrate it, interiorise it, absorb it into our very being. The word, as it were, enters our bloodstream and we allow it to nourish us in our depths. One may need to practise this form of prayer over time in order to discover its power to transform. At first, it may seem a busy way of prayer, but with practice one can learn the art of 'relishing the word' and releasing its power and energy into our lives.

Imbibing and inebriation

The bridegroom in the Song of Songs calls out: 'Eat, friends, drink, and be drunk with love' (5:1). Paul writes: 'Do not get drunk with wine... but be filled with the Spirit' (Ephesians 5:18). Gregory of Nyssa used the phrase 'sober inebriation' to describe a spiritual ecstasy that comes from drinking in God's love in the chalice of the Eucharist and in the course of virtuous living. Macarius the Great spoke of being 'intoxicated with God'[5] while Isaac the Syrian (613–700) tells of how God seizes the soul and leads the person into a state of divine madness, becoming a fool for Christ. In the Syriac, the term 'inebriation' is linked linguistically to the term wonder/ amazement:

> Sometimes, while prayer remains for its part, the intellect is taken away from it as if into heaven, and tears fall like fountains of waters, involuntarily soaking the whole face. All this time such a person is serene, still and filled with a wonder-filled vision... he remains continually in amazement at God's work

in creation – like people who are crazed by wine, for this is the 'wine which causes the person's heart to rejoice' (Psalm 104:15). Blessed is the person who has entered this door in the experience of his own soul, for all the power of ink, letters and phrases is too feeble to indicate the delight of this mystery.[6]

Bernard of Clairvaux wrote of 'that sober inebriation which comes not from drinking new wine but from enjoying God'. Mechthild of Magdeburg in her *Flowing Light of the Godhead* delights in the heady brew of divine love:

God lays the soul in his glowing heart so that He, the great God, and she, the humble maid, embrace and are united as thoroughly as water is with wine.[7]

In this 'cup of blessing', we taste rich imagery expressing the way God's grace stimulates and arouses us. Forgetting our sorrows, we rediscover the overwhelming joy of God.

A contemporary at the same convent at Helfta, Saxony, Gertrude the Great, in her *Spiritual Exercises* relates a vision of Christ in which he says to her soul:

Why are you troubled my love? For as often as you desire it, I, the sovereign priest and true pontiff, will enter you... I feed you with myself in the superfluity of my charity, and satisfy you with delights; and I penetrate your entire being like ointment by the sweetness of my spirit.[8]

St John of the Cross (b. 1542) in his *Spiritual Canticle* takes this imagery to new depths of intensity and passion. He sees the human–divine relationship moving from spiritual betrothal to spiritual marriage, union and consummation:

In the inner wine cellar
I drank of my Beloved ...

There he gave me his breast;
There he taught me a sweet and living knowledge;
I gave myself to him,
Keeping nothing back;
There I promised to be his bride.[9]

Spirituality of water

In the history of Christian spirituality, the image of water has inspired countless teachers of prayer. Let us look at two examples, drawn from east and west.

St Symeon the New Theologian (949–1022) is one of the eastern church's greatest mystics. He emphasises the necessity of personal encounter with the divine, and tells his own story:

> He led me by the hand as one leads a blind man to the fountain head, that is, to the holy scriptures and to Your divine commandments... One day when I was hurrying to plunge myself in this daily bath, You met me on the road, You who had already drawn me out of the mire. Then for the first time the pure light of Your divine face shone before my weak eyes... From that day on, You returned often at the fountain source, You would plunge my head into the water, letting me see the splendour of Your light... One day when it seemed as though You were plunging me over and over again in the lustral waters, lightning flashes surrounded me. I saw the rays from Your face merge with the waters; washed by these radiant waters, I was carried out of myself.[10]

For Symeon, the image of the waters becomes a powerful metaphor for the spiritual life, bespeaking the unfathomable resources of the Spirit and God's generosity in sharing his gifts. In the west, St Teresa of Avila (1515–82) confesses:

I cannot find anything more apt for the explanation of certain
spiritual things than this element of water; for, as I am ignorant
and my wit gives me no help and I am so fond of this element,
I have looked at it more attentively than at other things.[11]

She teaches about the Prayer of Quiet using the picture of the
fountain:

Let us suppose that we are looking at two fountains, the basins
of which can be filled with water… These two large basins can
be filled with water in different ways: the water in the one
comes from a long distance, by means of numerous conduits
and through human skill; but the other has been constructed
at the very source of the water and fills without making any
noise. If the flow of water is abundant, as in the case we are
speaking of, a great stream still runs from it after it has been
filled; no skill is necessary here, and no conduits have to be
made, for the water is flowing all the time. The difference
between this and the carrying of the water by means of
conduits is, I think, as follows. The latter corresponds to the
spiritual sweetness which, as I say, is produced by meditation.
It reaches us by way of the thoughts; we meditate upon
created things and fatigue the understanding; and when at
last, by means of our own efforts, it comes, the satisfaction
which it brings to the soul fills the basin, but in doing so makes
a noise, as I have said.
    To the other fountain the water comes direct from its
source, which is God, and, when it is His Majesty's will and He
is pleased to grant us some supernatural favour, its coming
is accompanied by the greatest peace and quietness and
sweetness within ourselves.[12]

In this passage from the *Interior Castle*, written in 1577, Teresa
suggests there are two ways of receiving the water of God. We can
stand at a distance from the fountain of God and receive the water
of the Spirit as it were mediated through man-made and lengthy

aqueducts and conduits, miles of pipelines of active, often noisy, talkative prayer. This, in fact, creates a distance from the fountain. Or, we can stand very close to the fountain of God, quieten our spirit and change our prayer from an active thinking and striving style to a more receptive, passive, drinking-in style. In what Teresa calls 'the Prayer of Quiet', we can drink directly and immediately of the river of the Spirit bubbling up in front of us. How close, she asks, are you to the fountain?

Rediscovering festivity

Brother Roger of Taizé cried out: 'Restore to pastors a spirit of festival!'[13] The local church needs to allow festivity to course through its lifeblood and should be famous, or even infamous, in the neighbourhood for the generosity of its welcome and its extraordinary embrace of the other. We must practise risky, open-hearted and costly hospitality that communicates the heart of the gospel more powerfully and effectively than a thousand sermons. Not a jolly parish social that is superficial but rather a healing and restorative gathering that generates acceptance of the outsider and balm to the wounded. We could learn from Christians in Latin America. Casaldaliga and Vigil write:

> A sort of 'state of fiesta' can be interwoven, in a logic that defies rules and prejudices, with work, suffering, prayer... Festivals are also pluriform expressions of meeting and communicating... of myths and memories, of eating and drinking, of faith and sensuality, of utopia and satire... a culture shock for those unable to understand the amalgam of mourning and laughing, drinking and believing, death and vitality, that these celebrations involve.[14]

The Eucharist reveals the church as it should be: a community of faith in which different gifts and ministries are exercised. The Eucharist can be a place of profound affirmation and vocation.

At the offertory, we place upon the holy table our gift of bread 'which earth has given and human hands have made'. This is a powerful symbol of God's call to us to surrender into his hands our daily work and labour. The wine that we bring forward and place on the table as an offering represents the surrender to God of both our sorrows and our joys. The chalice now holds 'wine to gladden the human heart' (Psalm 104:15) but also represents the cup of suffering (Mark 14:36). These elements of creation, embodying our sweat, our pain and our hope, invite us to live out daily in the world a Christian approach to creation, a sacramental view of the universe; seeing all creation as God-bearing and God-revealing.

By the power of the Holy Spirit, the natural elements of bread and wine become for us the body and blood of Christ: a powerful image of God's call to us to surrender into his hands the raw material of our lives, that we may become Christ-bearers for our needy world. We find ourselves caught up into the movement of Christ's self-offering to the Father, as we make *anamnesis* (remembrance) of the cross.

At the fraction, the action of the breaking of the bread, we see before our very eyes the clearest possible expression of the Christian life – to be consecrated for God and to be broken and given for the people: 'the bread that I will give for the life of the world' (John 6:51). In Holy Communion, we discover the presence of Christ, in some way, in fragments of broken bread and in poured-out wine. Then we must go out and discover Christ's presence in the broken bread of the sacrament of the poor: 'I was sick and you took care of me' (Matthew 25:36), finding Christ in fragmenting, fragile bread-like lives. The Eucharist, celebrating 'God with us' and 'the Word made flesh' in the physicality and materiality of created elements, prompts us to go out into God's world and become ever more alert to God's presence in human lives: to rediscover the sacramentality of all of life. St John Chrysostom asks:

> Do you wish to honour the body of Christ? Do not ignore him when he is naked. Do not pay him homage in the temple clad

in silk, only then to neglect him outside where he is cold and ill-clad. He who said: 'This is my body' is the same who said: 'You saw me hungry and you gave me no food', and 'whatever you did to the least of my brothers you did also to me...' What good is it if the Eucharistic table is overloaded with golden chalices when your brother is dying of hunger? Start by satisfying his hunger and then with what is left you may adorn the altar as well.[15]

As we enjoy the gift of Holy Communion, we recognise in this action a reminder of the call to go out into the world to respond to both the physical and the spiritual hunger: to feed the poor and the spiritually hungry of the earth.

Elements within the Eucharist can energise mission and remind us all of the celebratory and festive character of the banquet at the table of the kingdom, the altar of the Lord. At the very heart of the Eucharist is the joyous celebration of the cross, Passion and resurrection of the Lord. It is the paschal mystery, the mystery of Easter, the mystery of God's sharing and redeeming our human pain, that will help make sense of the daily practice of Christian living. What is proclaimed in the Eucharist – in both word and sacrament – is nothing less than the very message we will live out in our daily mission. The Eucharist clarifies and strengthens our vocation. The Eucharist is not just another service to attend, but a life to be lived, for in it, as in all worship, God invites us to formation and transformation by the Holy Spirit. The Eucharist powerfully reminds us, on each occasion, of our mission and vocation. Augustine puts it:

If you, therefore, are Christ's body and members, it is your own mystery that is placed on the Lord's table! It is your own mystery that you are receiving! You are saying 'Amen' to what you are: your response is a personal signature, affirming your faith. When you hear 'The Body of Christ' you reply 'Amen'. Be a member of Christ's body, that your 'Amen' may ring true![16]

We must ensure that every Eucharist is characterised by a blend of celebration and solidarity: every celebration should be life-affirming and life-empowering. The Eucharist should reflect the joyous meals of Jesus and his message of liberation and acceptance. Let fiesta break out! Brother Roger puts it:

> Festival is a small field that each of us has to cultivate within oneself, a tiny playground for exercising freedom and spontaneity… In every person lies a zone of solitude that no human intimacy can fill: and there God encounters us. There, in that depth, is set the intimate festival of the risen Christ. So henceforth, in the hollow of our being, we discover the risen Christ: he is our festival… the risen Christ makes of a person's life a continual festival.[17]

. . . .

Questions for reflection

1 'How sweet are your words to my taste, sweeter than honey to my mouth!' (Psalm 119:103). What does your God taste like?

2 How can we ensure that the sacred meal of the Eucharist highlights the themes of celebration, revelation and transformation?

3 Compose a 'grace' or prayer of thanksgiving you can use at the beginning of a meal that picks up on the Johannine themes we have looked at.

4 What steps can you take to 'live festivity'?

Prayer exercise

Either
Prepare a simple agape meal, using aromatic (maybe Indian?) elements that you can savour slowly and appreciatively.

Or
Celebrate a contemplative Eucharist with freshly baked bread and fine wine. Use the prayer from the first-century *Didache*:

> As the grain once scattered in the fields
> and the grapes once dispersed on the hillside
> are now reunited on this table in bread and wine,
> so, Lord, may your whole church soon be gathered together
> from the corners of the earth
> into your kingdom!

9

Welcoming the aroma of heaven

Throughout the fourth gospel, John evokes a range of sensory experiences of smell. Throughout the narrative, John stimulates the nostrils of imagination. As we see Jesus driving cattle, sheep and doves from the temple precincts (John 2), we catch a whiff of the earthy, natural, pungent pongs of the animals. In the same chapter, we sense the sweet, inebriating bouquet of the wine.

Maybe we sense the very perspiration of Jesus, as the gospel explicitly tells us that he was exhausted by his journey and placed himself by Jacob's Well in the sweltering heat of the midday sun. In chapter 8, can we avoid catching a whiff of a telltale musky scent from the woman described graphically as *in flagrante delicto* ('taken in adultery')?

Chapter 6 invites us to inhale the smell of the grass on the hillside, specifically mentioned, newly broken bread and indeed the wind blowing in our faces – 'a strong wind was blowing' (6:18).

We experience the crackle of charcoal fire where Peter warms himself in the courtyard of the high priest (18:18). We can almost smell the sponge full of pungent vinegar offered to Jesus on the cross (19:29).

The Easter story is fragrant with scent, as we shall see. In John 21, as we hear the sputtering of the charcoal fire that the risen Christ has prepared on the beach, our appetites are whetted by the tantalising scent of sizzling fish and the intoxicating aroma of fresh bread, bread to be torn, broken and given.

The stench of death

John offers us an alternative Martha/Mary story. In Luke, Mary is the contemplative, sitting at the feet of Jesus, while Martha represents the active, busy preparing meals. In John, we meet Mary and Martha in connection with the sense of smell, but it is not the smell of cooking!

First, we encounter Martha, ever the practical one, at the tomb of Lazarus. Jesus has delayed his visit to Bethany and arrives after the death of Lazarus and his entombment. As he asks that the stone be moved away from the mouth of the cave-tomb, 'Martha, the sister of the dead man, said to him, "Lord, already there is a stench because he has been dead for four days"' (11:39). She fears that nostrils will be assaulted by the rancid, retching whiff of death, the foul odour and stink of decay. Martha experiences a sense of repulsion as she considers the pungent decomposition of her brother's corpse, the acrid putrefying of his cadaver, the rank, reeking scent of mortality. She is daunted by the very thought of an expected nauseating, noxious, polluting smell. But Jesus sees not disaster but the potential for the glory of God to break out in this situation.

The aroma of life

In contrast, we encounter Mary as she offers Jesus an exuberant, extravagant, fragrant act of adoration. It borders on the scandalous and outrageous, for she is crossing boundaries as she not only anoints the feet of Jesus with expensive perfume but also wipes his feet with her hair: 'Mary took a pound of costly perfume made of pure nard, anointed Jesus' feet, and wiped them with her hair.' John adds the sensory note: 'The house was filled with the fragrance of the perfume' (12:3). Unfettered, a sweet scent from the expensive aromatic oils fills the air and wafts into the nostrils. The profusion of the perfume pervades, permeates every corner of the house, drifts through the air and percolates through every level.[1] It is a heady, intoxicating, life-giving aroma: the scent of eternity. Jesus understands her gesture of pouring a great quantity of perfume on to his feet both as an act of honour and as a sign that his body is soon to be buried. Judas estimates the worth of the perfume as 300 denarii. A denarius represents the daily wage for a labourer. In today's value, that anointing would cost approximately £20,000!

John's gospel invites us to learn deeply from Mary's extravagant act at Bethany of pouring perfume on the feet of Jesus about the character of worship. This episode challenges us to offer worship that is costly, sacrificial. We are moved to 'give and not to count the cost'. Our worship might be as sacramental and expressive as Mary's act of devotion. We are summoned to offer worship that is generous and extravagant, holding nothing back. Indeed, might our worship be like Mary's perfume, 'filling the whole house with its fragrance' – and having an effect way beyond the sanctuary?

The fragrance of the risen Jesus

On the first Easter morning, when Mary Magdalene encounters Jesus, she will be struck by the extraordinary fragrance he exudes. The newly risen Jesus appears in a haze of perfume, glistening, shimmering, gleaming, steaming with life-giving scent. Just before sundown on Good Friday, Joseph of Arimathea had obtained Pilate's permission to remove the body of Jesus from the cross and place it in a nearby rock-cut tomb. John tells us:

> He came and removed his body. Nicodemus, who had at first come to Jesus by night, also came, bringing a mixture of myrrh and aloes, weighing about a hundred pounds. They took the body of Jesus and wrapped it with the spices in linen cloths, according to the burial custom of the Jews.
> JOHN 19:38–40

The body of Jesus is now anointed with a vast, outrageously extravagant amount of myrrh and aloes – one hundred pounds in weight – an extraordinary quantity, said to be enough for 200 persons. The earth has offered to Jesus spices crushed from resins, releasing an extraordinary, balmy fragrance. As the risen Jesus meets Mary Magdalene in a haze and aura of spices, he will be dripping with a moist, tantalising and mysterious elixir – he will be literally sensational.

The reference in John's gospel evokes the messianic psalm:

> You are the fairest of the sons of men;
>> grace is poured upon your lips;
>> therefore God has blessed you for ever...
> Your robes are all fragrant with myrrh and aloes and cassia.
> PSALM 45:2, 8 (RSV)

As we noted, scholars have detected in John's account of the Easter meeting with Mary Magdalene many allusions to and echoes from the Song of Songs, the great love poem at the heart of the Bible. First, you recall, there is the garden. John is at pains to point out: 'Now there was a garden in the place where he was crucified, and in the garden there was a new tomb in which no one had ever been laid' (19:41). Indeed, when Mary first encounters the risen Lord, she mistakes him for the gardener. This is an echo of Eden, the garden of paradise – a new creation is beginning. It is an allusion to the luxuriant environment in which the love poem of the Song of Songs is set.

There, the lover says of her beloved: 'His cheeks are like beds of spices, yielding fragrance. His lips are lilies, distilling liquid myrrh' (Song of Songs 5:13), while the Lover delights in the fragrances of his beloved:

> You have ravished my heart, my sister, my bride,
>> you have ravished my heart with a glance of your eyes,
>> with one jewel of your necklace.

How sweet is your love, my sister, my bride!
  how much better is your love than wine,
  and the fragrance of your oils than any spice!
Your lips distil nectar, my bride;
  honey and milk are under your tongue;
  the scent of your garments is like the scent of Lebanon.
A garden locked is my sister, my bride,
  a garden locked, a fountain sealed.
Your channel is an orchard of pomegranates
  with all choicest fruits,
  henna with nard,
nard and saffron, calamus and cinnamon,
  with all trees of frankincense,
myrrh and aloes,
  with all chief spices –
a garden fountain, a well of living water,
  and flowing streams from Lebanon.
Awake, O north wind,
  and come, O south wind!
Blow upon my garden
  that its fragrance may be wafted abroad.
SONG OF SONGS 4:9–16

The great Johannine scholar Raymond Brown notes that John's use of myrrh and aloes at Jesus' tomb is an unusual combination of spices, as aloe is not normally used at burials. However, it is precisely to this combination that the Song of Songs refers, in the passage here, the final description of the lover as a 'garden of spices'.[2] John is once again deliberately evoking the eroticism of the Song of Songs.

James B. Nelson observes of the garden of the Song of Songs:

Here, surely, is God's gift of the erotic. Here is love with passion and heart, love that is warm and moist, love that searches for fulfilment in both giving and receiving. Here is our hunger to taste and smell, to see and touch. Here is the flow of our senses, the sacred power of our desire. Without all of this, love as sacrifice and self-giving becomes cold. Without this, the world itself becomes hard and metallic.

And, thinking of John's gospel, he asks:

> Can God's own love be erotic? Not a dispassionate, self-sufficient deity dispensing divine favour to helpless humans, but the Lover yearning, seeking, desiring? Can that be true? 'In the beginning was the Word' (John 1:1). When that Word came to dwell with us, it became no abstract doctrine, no sacred book, no code of morality. It became flesh. Jesus, to the horror of squeamish Christians, was a laughing, crying, sweating, eating, drinking... sensuous bundle of flesh just as we are... there is the good news! God embraces human flesh as the fitting vehicle of divine presence... Might we still 'behold that glory'?[3]

Above all, John's gospel heartens us: the stench of death and the horror of crucifixion give way to the scent of the intoxicating, energising, life-giving aroma of the resurrection, the unbridled fragrance of the Easter garden.

· · · · · · · · · · · · · · · · · ·

Spirituality of scent

Fragrant aromatic substances, including ointments, anointing oils and incense, are mentioned throughout the Old Testament. Proverbs 27:9 declares: 'Perfume and incense make the heart glad.' Fragrances especially occur in the context of worship as something that can be offered to God. Moses is instructed by God to use the finest fragrances on the altar of incense in the tabernacle: 'Take sweet spices, stacte, and onycha, and galbanum, sweet spices with pure frankincense (an equal part of each), and make an incense blended as by the perfumer, seasoned with salt, pure and holy' (Exodus 30:34–35). The Hebrew word translated 'perfume' comes about 58 times in the Old Testament, often translated as 'sweet incense'. In addition, the use of anointing oils is celebrated:

> Take the finest spices: of liquid myrrh five hundred shekels, and of sweet-smelling cinnamon half as much, that is, two hundred fifty, and two hundred fifty of aromatic cane, and five hundred of cassia – measured by the sanctuary shekel – and a hin of olive oil; and you shall make of these a sacred anointing-oil blended as by the perfumer; it shall be a holy anointing-oil.
> EXODUS 30:23–25

We might be familiar with the words from Psalm 23:5:

> You prepare a table before me
>   in the presence of my enemies;
> you anoint my head with oil;
>   my cup overflows.

The Christian tradition has delighted in the sense of smell.[4] When the early church father Origen (182–254) sought a metaphor for Christ's love, he turned to the world of smell and perfume:

> When souls... have experienced the pleasantness of [Christ's] sweetness and odour, when they have received the fragrance

of His ointments and have grasped at last the reason for His coming, the motives of the Redemption and Passion, and the love whereby He, the Immortal, went even to the death of the cross for the salvation of all men, then these maiden souls, attracted by all this as by the odours of a divine and ineffable perfume and being filled with vigour and complete alacrity, run after Him and hasten to the odour of His sweetness, not at a slow pace, nor with lagging steps, but swiftly and with all the speed they can.[5]

In the fourth century, St Ephrem the Syrian celebrated the natural world as 'a vast censer':

exhaling fragrance
impregnates the air
with its odoriferous smoke,
imparting to all who are near it
a whiff from which to benefit.
How much the more so
with Paradise the glorious:
even its fence assists us,
modifying somewhat
that curse upon the earth
by the scent of its aromas.[6]

He suggests that we can catch the scents of eternity and the fragrance of Paradise, here below, in daily life – if our senses are alert enough!

In the Orthodox church, oil plays a significant role. In the Armenian tradition, for example, the sanctified oil of holy *muron* is consecrated every seven years in Armenia and distributed to parishes across the globe. *Muron* is a Greek word meaning 'fragrant oil' or 'essence flowing from a plant'. The word is derived from the root 'to rub', 'to anoint'. It is composed of olive oil together with various fragrant spices.

In the Orthodox tradition, the holy *muron* is used for Chrismation, which is conducted immediately after baptism. The candidate is anointed in Christ and receives the Holy Spirit. The priest anoints the forehead, eyes, ears, nostrils, mouth, hands, heart, back and feet with holy *muron*, and prays to God to bestow the gift of the Holy Spirit so that the recipient may live in righteousness and follow the Light of God. (Holy Communion is given for the first time after the anointing, where the candidate becomes a full member of the Body of Christ.) This use of the oil teaches that God honours and consecrates all the senses of the body – with them, the candidate is ready to discover God throughout the journey of life!

. . . .

Questions for reflection

1 What strikes you from this chapter? What do your reactions tell you about your heart's desire?

2 If you were describing the nature and impact of your church, what kind of scent would come to mind?

3 What kind of scent does your life give off, metaphorically? What ingredients contribute to it?

4 What is your response to James Nelson's question, 'Can God's own love be erotic?'

Prayer exercises

Either

The sacrifice of Jesus is a sweet-smelling offering

Burn incense on some charcoal or light a joss stick. Read quietly: 'Live in love, as Christ loved us and gave himself up for us, a fragrant offering and sacrifice to God' (Ephesians 5:2).

Notice how the smoke goes *up* to heaven. As you look at this and enjoy the scent, reflect on Christ's generous self-offering, his utter giving of himself to the Father 'for the life of the world' (John 6). Sing (or play from YouTube) this song:

> May the fragrance of Jesus fill this place. (*Men*)
> May the fragrance of Jesus fill this place. (*Women*)
> May the fragrance of Jesus fill this place. (*Men*)
> Lovely fragrance of Jesus, (*Women*)
> Rising from the sacrifice (*All*)
> Of lives laid down in adoration.
>
> May the glory of Jesus fill His church. (*Men*)
> May the glory of Jesus fill His church. (*Women*)
> May the glory of Jesus fill His church. (*Men*)
> Radiant glory of Jesus, (*Women*)
> Shining from our faces (*All*)
> As we gaze in adoration.
>
> May the beauty of Jesus fill my life. (*Men*)
> May the beauty of Jesus fill my life. (*Women*)
> May the beauty of Jesus fill my life. (*Men*)
> Perfect beauty of Jesus, (*Women*)
> Fill my thoughts, my words, my deeds, (*All*)
> My all I give in adoration.
> Graham Kendrick[7]

Conclude with a time of open prayer and self-offering, prefaced by the scripture:

Another angel with a golden censer came and stood at the altar; he was given a great quantity of incense to offer with the prayers of all the saints on the golden altar that is before the throne. And the smoke of the incense, with the prayers of the saints, rose before God from the hand of the angel.
REVELATION 8:3–4

Or

We are the fragrance of Christ

Place in a bowl fragrant fruits, such as lemons, oranges or apples, or a collection of flowers, leaves or fresh herbs, such as rosemary, basil or lavender. Pass the bowl around the group, inviting each person to select one item. Allow time to enjoy the citrus scents or other fragrances. Allow your nostrils to tingle!

In the silence, read the scripture slowly:

I arose to open to my beloved,
    and my hands dripped with myrrh,
my fingers with liquid myrrh,
    upon the handles of the bolt.
I opened to my beloved…
My beloved is all radiant and ruddy,
    distinguished among ten thousand…
His cheeks are like beds of spices,
    yielding fragrance.
His lips are lilies,
    distilling liquid myrrh…
This is my beloved and this is my friend.
SONG OF SONGS 5: 5–6, 10, 13, 16

How would you describe the fragrance of Christ?

Then read:

> But thanks be to God, who... through us spreads in every place the fragrance that comes from knowing him. For we are the aroma of Christ.
> 2 CORINTHIANS 2:14–15

> I have been paid in full and have more than enough; I am fully satisfied, now that I have received from Epaphroditus the gifts you sent, a fragrant offering, a sacrifice acceptable and pleasing to God.
> PHILIPPIANS 4:18

What kind of fragrance or scent do you bring to others?

Conclude by silently and deliberately crushing one item to release its full aroma through its brokenness.

Pray that you too may be broken and given for others in need.

You may like to include an anointing in your prayer reflection. If in a group, you could trace the sign of the cross on one another's palms with a suitable fragrant oil (such as lavender or eucalyptus) as a sign of consecrating our hands to God's service and to the service of one another.

10

Reawakening:
life in all its fullness

In this chapter, we conclude by celebrating John's central message:
by encountering the Word, we are invited to taste life in all its fullness.
We see that, in the fourth gospel, Jesus brings a truth that sets us
free: it is liberating, empowering, releasing us from captivities and
things that hold us down, so we can be become fully alive in Christ.
Discovering in the Jesus of the fourth gospel a human flourishing, a
spiritual blossoming, we reflect how we can share this with others.

Coming fully alive

Knowing the Hebrew scriptures so well, John was familiar with
Psalm 115, which contrasts the living, active God with idols that have
no senses:

> Their idols are silver and gold,
>> the work of human hands.
> They have mouths, but do not speak;
>> eyes, but do not see.
> They have ears, but do not hear;
>> noses, but do not smell.
> They have hands, but do not feel;
>> feet, but do not walk…
> Those who make them are like them;
>> so are all who trust in them.
>
> PSALM 115:4–8

To be alive is to be alert with the senses; to be dead is to have no faculties of response. John's God is himself all-hearing and all-knowing:

> He who planted the ear, does he not hear?
> He who formed the eye, does he not see?
> PSALM 94:9

Indeed, the God of the Hebrew scriptures is the very source of the senses. Proverbs puts it so succinctly:

> The hearing ear and the seeing eye –
>   the Lord has made them both.
> PROVERBS 20:12

John stands in a tradition which believes that the senses are God-given gifts to be enjoyed. Indeed, the very mission of Israel was expressed in terms of activating the senses. John knew the prophet Isaiah (which, as we noted, he quotes), and the Servant Songs of Isaiah have influenced the fourth gospel in various ways. They express the mission of the servant in terms of opening of eyes:

> Here is my servant, whom I uphold,
>   my chosen, in whom my soul delights…
> I am the Lord, I have called you in righteousness,
>   I have taken you by the hand and kept you;
> I have given you as a covenant to the people,
>   a light to the nations,
>   to open the eyes that are blind,
> to bring out the prisoners from the dungeon,
>   from the prison those who sit in darkness.
> ISAIAH 42:1, 6–7

'The glory of God is a human being fully alive!'

In making this affirmation, Irenaeus might be summing up John's gospel, which he loved so deeply. In his gospel, John celebrates the life-giving, living God. In the Word made flesh, the divine presence becomes palpable, tangible, verifiable. The Word is discovered through all the senses. John sums up his gospel in the words he places on Jesus' lips: 'I came that they may have life, and have it abundantly' (10:10). This is life in all its exuberance. The Greek word *perissos* means 'above measure, more than average, above the common, extraordinary, more than sufficient, with a surplus'. The AMPC puts it: 'I came that they may have *and* enjoy life, and have it in abundance, to the full, till it overflows.' Jesus offers life in its fullest measure, life that is full and good. *The Message* gives us: 'I came so they can have real and eternal life, more and better life than they ever dreamed of.' The NLV renders this: 'I came so they might have life, a great full life.' This is expressed so poignantly in Jesus' exhilarating first sign: the wine of Cana – luscious, intoxicating – is a sign of God's extravagant, overflowing love shown to us in Jesus, a love we are invited to plunge ourselves into and share with others.

Mission in John's gospel

It is significant that John expresses our call to mission in three tactile, visceral images:

'Wash one another's feet'

Cascading water splashing over dirty feet, a gurgling stream of cleansing water – this is the first symbol of our mission: 'So if I, your Lord and Teacher, have washed your feet, you also ought to wash one another's feet. For I have set you an example, that you also should do as I have done to you' (13:14–15). The splash of water sweeping away clogging dust and dirt, bringing renewal – this visceral image expresses humbly yet powerfully the call to share the divine life, to restore the weary, to refresh anew the downhearted. Feet might now be honoured: as Isaiah puts it:

> How beautiful upon the mountains
>   are the feet of the messenger who announces peace,
> who brings good news,
>   who announces salvation,
>   who says to Zion, 'Your God reigns.'
> ISAIAH 52:7

This foot-washing symbol of mission is about acceptance, welcome. But it is also about honouring others, and recognising and affirming their true potential. Feet, once washed, can go out again into the world!

'Bear much fruit'

> I am the vine, you are the branches. Those who abide in me and I in them bear much fruit, because apart from me you can do nothing... My Father is glorified by this, that you bear much fruit and become my disciples.
> JOHN 15:5, 8

The divine vintner and vine-grower is looking for luxuriance: 'more fruit', 'much fruit' (15:2, 5). To the extent that we allow the divine life to flow through us, like sap rising in a vine, we will produce a bumper harvest of luscious grapes. This mouth-watering image conveys a life-giving mission. We are being called to be juicy, delightful, attractive, like grapes dangling tantalisingly on the vine waiting to be savoured and enjoyed. In the background lies this suggestively erotic passage about *Sophia* or Wisdom in Ecclesiasticus 24:

> I spread out my branches,
>   and my branches are glorious and graceful.
> Like the vine I bud forth delights,
>   and my blossoms become glorious and abundant fruit.

'Come to me, you who desire me,
　　and eat your fill of my fruits.
For the memory of me is sweeter than honey,
　　and the possession of me sweeter than the honeycomb.
Those who eat of me will hunger for more,
　　and those who drink of me will thirst for more.'
ECCLESIASTICUS 24:16–21

'Receive the Holy Spirit'

In the upper room on Easter Day, the risen Christ reveals himself with an astonishing physicality. Not only does he show them wounded, scarred hands and feet, but he goes further. He opens his mouth wide and, with a great exhalation of spirit, 'he breathed on them and said to them, "Receive the Holy Spirit"' (20:22).

What was the experience like? The disciples felt the warm breath of Jesus on their faces. In their souls, they felt an extraordinary sense of infilling, empowering. This is John's Pentecost: both the commissioning of the disciples and their fuelling: 'As the Father has sent me, so I send you' (20:21). Disciples become apostles in this moment. And one aspect of the sending is highlighted: 'If you forgive the sins of any, they are forgiven them; if you retain the sins of any, they are retained' (20:23). The apostles have the power to accept others or reject them, to extend or withhold forgiveness.

In order to receive this threefold commission, the disciples have to do but one thing: they have to open their senses as wide as possible. They need a wide-eyed wakefulness. Their mission is communicated and received in the feel of cold water on sweaty feet, the visualisation of dangling succulent grapes, the experience of a breath upon their faces. Peter's question and protest sums up our resistance: 'Lord, are you going to wash my feet?… You will never wash my feet' (13:6, 8). Maybe you too have felt reluctant to respond, in reading this book, hesitant about engaging unreservedly?

Maybe Jesus' response to Peter is appropriate for us too: 'You do not know now what I am doing, but later you will understand' (13:7). 'Later': it is only after we have stood at the cross and glimpsed the body of Jesus steaming with sweat and running with blood; only after we encounter, with Mary Magdalene, the glistening, fragrant body of the risen Christ; only then can we realise that the gospel is sensational, sensitising, sensuous, indeed. And only when we have touched and handled the Word of life in all his manifestations; only when we have imbibed his wine and caught the whisper of his voice in the breeze; only when we have glimpsed the presence of God in the scars of human woundedness and in the springtime of the planet; only then can we exult with John: 'And the Word became flesh and lived among us, and we have seen his glory!'

. . . .

Questions for reflection

1   What contributes to your thriving and flourishing as a Christian? What erodes or undermines this?

2   What positive, creative steps can you take in order to enjoy the divine life flowing into you more and more?

3   In what ways are you presently sharing the good news with others, as John did?

4   In what ways might you more daringly fulfil the three aspects of mission highlighted in this chapter? Go for it!

Prayer exercise

Conclude with a multisensory Eucharist or, if you are on your own, prepare a simple yet sensuous meal. Activate all the senses: for sight, light candles or use icons; for smell, use incense or joss sticks. For the sense of touch, remember how important the sign of peace is in the Eucharist and share this in an unrushed way (perhaps by hugging). Incorporate the renewal of baptism vows, with generous sprinkling of water, or come up one by one to a large bowl of water and immerse hands or make the sign of the cross with it. If possible, after the commission below, receive anointing with the fragrant oil of chrism used at baptism, confirmation and ordination. Choose as your gospel reading a passage that has stood out for you from this book.

> Friends, God has touched you with his love
> and given you a place among his people.
> God promises to be with you
> in joy and in sorrow,
> to be your guide in life,
> and to bring you safely to heaven.

> In baptism, God invites you on a lifelong journey.
> Together with all God's people
> you must explore the way of Jesus
> and grow in friendship with God,
> in love for his people,
> and in serving others.
> With us you will listen to the word of God
> and receive the gifts of God.

> Those who are baptised are called to worship and serve God.
> Will you continue in the apostles' teaching and fellowship,
> in the breaking of bread, and in the prayers?
> **With the help of God, I will.**

Will you persevere in resisting evil,
and, whenever you fall into sin, repent and return to the Lord?
With the help of God, I will.

Will you proclaim by word and example
the good news of God in Christ?
With the help of God, I will.

Will you seek and serve Christ in all people,
loving your neighbour as yourself?
With the help of God, I will.

Will you acknowledge Christ's authority over human society,
by prayer for the world and its leaders,
by defending the weak, and by seeking peace and justice?
With the help of God, I will.

May Christ dwell in your hearts through faith,
that you may be rooted and grounded in love
and bring forth the fruit of the Spirit.[1]

Notes

Introduction

1 Andrew D. Mayes, *Holy Land: Challenging questions from the biblical landscape* (SPCK, 2011); *Beyond the Edge: Spiritual transitions for adventurous souls* (SPCK, 2013). See also Andrew D. Mayes, *Journey to the Centre of the Soul: A handbook for explorers* (BRF, 2017), which takes the reader underground in the Holy Land.

2 The puzzles concerning the authorship of the fourth gospel are well documented, as well as the issue of the evangelist as an eyewitness. See, for example, Stephen S. Smalley, *John: Evangelist and interpreter* (Paternoster, 1978); Gary M. Burge, *Interpreting the Gospel of John* (Baker, 1992), pp. 37–54; D.A. Carson, *The Gospel According to John* (Inter-Varsity Press; Eerdmans, 1991).

3 Irenaeus, *Against Heresies*, III.3:4.

4 Maryanne M. Thompson, *Humanity of Jesus in the Fourth Gospel* (Fortress Press, 1988).

5 Cyril of Alexandria, *Commentary on John*, LFC 43, 48 (1874/1885) Praefatio. pp. 1–5.

6 Maurice F. Wiles, *Spiritual Gospel: The interpretation of the fourth gospel in the early church* (Cambridge University Press, 2008).

7 Origen, 'Commentary on the gospel of John, Book 1:9' in A. Roberts (ed.), *Ante-Nicene Fathers: Writings from the Fathers down to AD325* (Cosimo Classics, 2007).

8 Augustine, 'The harmony of the gospels 1.6.9' in *Nicene and Post-Nicene Fathers*, Vol. 6 (1885).

9 Augustine, *Harmony of the Gospels*, 1.6.9.

10 Richard Rohr, *The Naked Now: Learning to see as the mystics see* (Crossroad, 2009), p. 77.

11 R. Alan Culpepper, *Anatomy of the Fourth Gospel: A study in literary design* (Fortress Press, 1987).

12 Jeffrey L. Staley, *The Print's First Kiss: A rhetorical investigation of the implied reader in the fourth gospel* (Scholars Press, 1988).

Chapter 1 Unleashing the senses: the Word made flesh

1 *The Holy Scriptures according to the Masoretic Text: A new translation* (Jewish Publication Society, 1917).
2 Niels H. Gregersen (ed.), *Incarnation: On the scope and depth of Christology* (Fortress Press, 2015).
3 Elizabeth A. Johnson, 'Jesus and the cosmos: soundings in deep Christology' in Gregersen, *Incarnation*, p. 138.
4 Dorothy A. Lee, *Flesh and Glory: Symbolism, gender and theology in the gospel of John* (Crossroad, 2002), p. 48.
5 Kathleen E. McVey, *Ephrem the Syrian: Hymns* (Paulist Press, 1989).
6 Herbert Musurillo (tr.), *From Glory to Glory: Texts from Gregory of Nyssa's mystical writings* (John Murray, 1962), p. 156.
7 Henry Chadwick (tr.), *Saint Augustine: Confessions* (University Press, 1991), p. 201.
8 Jürgen Moltmann, *A Broad Place: An autobiography* (Fortress Press, 2008), p. 350.
9 Quoted in Matthew Fox, *Whee! We Wee All the Way Home: A guide to sensual, prophetic spirituality* (Bear and Company, 1981), p. 15.
10 See, for example, Joseph M. Stoutzenberger and John D. Bohrer, *Praying with Francis of Assisi* (Saint Mary's Press, 1989).
11 David Abram, *The Spell of the Sensuous* (Vintage Books, 1997), p. 268.
12 Maria A. Habig (ed.), *St Francis of Assisi: Writings and early biographies: Omnibus of the sources for the life of St Francis* (SPCK, 1979), p. 67.
13 'The Life of Saint Francis by Thomas of Celano' in R. Armstrong et al., *Francis of Assisi, Early Documents*, Vol. 1 (New City Press, 1999), p. 283.
14 Carlo Carretto, *I, Francis* (Fount, 1982), p. 130.
15 Edwin Cousins (tr.), *Bonaventure: The soul's journey into God* (Paulist Press, 1978), p. 70.
16 Cousins, *Bonaventure*, p. 67.
17 Cousins, *Bonaventure*, p. 73.
18 Cousins, *Bonaventure*, p. 89.
19 Edmund Colledge and James Walsh (trs), *Julian of Norwich: Showings* (Paulist Press, 1978), pp. 287, 289. Grace M. Jantzen points out that, for Julian, sensuality involves the union of soul and body, of consciousness with embodiment. See *Julian of Norwich: Mystic and theologian* (Paulist Press, 1988), p. 143.
20 Colledge and Walsh, *Julian*, p. 295.
21 Colledge and Walsh, *Julian*, p. 255.

22 Anthony Mottola (tr.), *The Spiritual Exercises of St Ignatius* (Image/ Doubleday, 1964).
23 Later, we shall explore possible links between the fourth gospel and the Song of Songs.
24 Musurillo, *From Glory to Glory*.
25 Marilyn Sewell (ed.), *Cries of the Spirit: A celebration of women's spirituality* (Beacon Press, 1991), p. 3. See Philip Sheldrake, *Befriending our Desires* (Darton, Longman & Todd, 2012).
26 Halcyon Backhouse (ed.), *The Song of Songs: Sections from the sermons of St Bernard of Clairvaux* (Hodder & Stoughton, 1990), p. 38.
27 Richard of St Victor, 'The four degrees of violent charity' in Hugh Feiss (ed.), *On Love*, Vol. 2 'The Victorine texts in translation' (New York City Press, 2012).
28 Matthew Fox (tr.), *Meditations with Meister Eckhart* (Bear & Co., 1983), pp. 88, 81.
29 Columbo Hart (tr.), *Hadewijch: The Complete Works* (Paulist Press, 1980), p. 165. See also Grace M. Jantzen, *Power, Gender and Christian Mysticism* (Cambridge University Press, 1995) and John Giles Milhaven, *Hadewijch and Her Sisters* (State University of New York Press, 1993).
30 John Donne, *Holy Sonnets* (1633), 140.
31 John Donne, *Holy Sonnets*, 18.
32 Thomas Traherne, *Centuries* (Faith Press, 1960), p. 112.
33 Thomas Merton, quoted in Esther de Waal, *A Seven Day Journey with Thomas Merton* (Eagle, 2000), p. 20.
34 David Steindl-Rast OSB, 'Encounter with God through the senses' in B. Shields and R. Carlson (eds.), *For the Love of God: Handbook for the spirit* (New World Library, 1997).

Chapter 2 Deep knowing: a sense of the divine

1 C.K. Barrett, *The Gospel According to St John* (SPCK, 1955), p. 31.
2 John Marsh, *Saint John (Pelican New Testament Commentary)* (Penguin, 1968), p. 34.
3 A.M. Hunter, *According to John* (SCM, 1968), p. 26.
4 C.H. Dodd, *The Interpretation of the Fourth Gospel* (Cambridge University Press, 1953), pp. 152, 154.
5 Yael Avrahami, *The Senses of Scripture: Sensory perception in the Hebrew Bible* (T and T Clark, 2012), p. 221, 162.
6 Libreria Editrice Vaticana, *Catechism of the Catholic Church* (Chapman, 1994), p. 545.

7   Quoted in Church Union, *Order for the Eucharist 2015* (Tufton Books, 2015), p. 39.
8   See Hans Walter Wolff, *Anthropology of the Old Testament* (SCM, 1974).
9   James Gaffney, 'Believing and knowing in the fourth gospel', *Theological Studies* (May 1965), 26:215–41.
10 Dumitru Stăniloae, *Orthodox Spirituality* (St Tikhon's Seminary Press, 2002), p. 209.
11 *Rule of Benedict*, Prologue.
12 Kallistos Ware, *The Inner Kingdom* (St Vladimir's Seminary Press, 2000), p. 62.
13 Kallistos Ware, 'Ways of prayer and contemplation I: eastern' in B. McGinn, J. Meyendorf and J. Leclerq, *Christian Spirituality: Origins to the 12th century* (SCM, 1985), p. 401.
14 Attributed to Simeon the New Theologian, 'Three methods of attention and prayer' in E. Kadloubovsky and G.E.H. Palmer, *Writings From the Philokalia* (Faber & Faber, 1977), p. 158.
15 Maximos the Confessor, 'Four hundred texts on love' in G.E.H. Palmer, P. Sherrard and K. Ware (trs.), *The Philokalia*, Volume 2 (Faber & Faber, 1981), p. 69.
16 Palmer, Sherrard and Ware, *Philokalia*, Volume 2, p. 74.
17 John Meyendorff, *Byzantine Theology: Historical trends and doctrinal themes* (Mowbray, 1975), p. 77.
18 John Meyendorff, *Gregory Palamas: The triads* (Paulist Press, 1983), p. 58.
19 Quoted in Andrew Louth, *Theology and Spirituality* (SLG Press, 2000), p. 4.
20 Interview with Fr Matthew, Vatopedi Monastery, Mount Athos, 29 May 2006.
21 Jürgen Moltmann, *The Spirit of Life: A universal affirmation* (SCM, 1992).
22 John Macquarrie, *Paths in Spirituality* (SCM, 1972), p. 34.
23 Rowan Williams, *Teresa of Avila* (Continuum, 1991), p. 156.
24 Fraser Watts and Mark Williams, *The Psychology of Religious Knowing* (Chapman, 1988), p. 115.
25 Watts and Williams, *Religious Knowing*, p. 113.
26 Ann and Barry Ulanov, *Primary Speech: A psychology of prayer* (John Knox Press, 1982), p. 122. See also experiences of God as understood as perception in W.P. Alson, *Perceiving God: The epistemology of religious experience* (Cornell University Press, 1991).

27 See, for example, Philip Sheldrake (ed.), *The Way of Ignatius Loyola: Contemporary approaches to the spiritual exercises* (SPCK, 1991).

28 David J. Hassel, *Radical Prayer* (Paulist Press, 1984).

29 Hassel, *Radical Prayer*, p. 8.

30 See, for example, Alasdair MacIntyre, *After Virtue: A study in moral theory* (Duckworth, 1985); Jean Porter, *The Recovery of Virtue* (SPCK, 1994); Christopher Cocksworth, *Wisdom: The Spirit's gift* (Grove Books, 2003).

31 David F. Ford, *The Shape of Living* (Fount, 1997), p. 72.

32 Andrew Louth, 'Theology, contemplation and the university', *Studies in Christian Ethics*, 17:1 (2004), pp. 69–79.

33 Mary Midgley, *Wisdom, Information and Wonder: What is knowledge for?* (Routledge, 1989), p. 19.

34 Midgley, *Wisdom*, p. 253.

35 Daniel W. Hardy, *God's Ways with the World* (T & T Clark, 1996), pp. 244–45.

36 David F. Ford and Daniel W. Hardy, *Living in Praise: Worshipping and knowing God* (DLT, 2005), p. 142.

37 Simeon the New Theologian, 'Practical and theological precepts' in Kadloubovsky and Palmer, *Writings From the Philokalia*, p. 130.

Chapter 3 Relocating: a sense of place

1 Bruce E. Schein, *Following the Way: The setting of John's gospel* (Augsburg Publishing House, 1980), pp. 7–8.

2 For scholarly articles, see R. Reich, E. Shukron and O. Lernau, 'Recent discoveries in the city of David, Jerusalem', *Israel Exploration Journal*, 57 (2007), pp. 153–68; Doron Ben-Ami and Yana Tchekhanovets, 'The lower city of Jerusalem on the eve of its destruction, 70 CE', *Bulletin of the American Schools of Oriental Research*, 364 (2011), pp. 61–85.

3 For Christians, the Pool of Siloam evokes the liminal waters of baptism, an important theme in John's gospel.

4 John links the gift of the Spirit to the paschal mystery. At the crucifixion, a fountain of eternal life is opened for humanity: as his side is pierced, blood and water stream out (John 19:34; compare 1 John 5:6–8). After Jesus is glorified on the cross, the Spirit can gush.

5 'The water drawing ceremony' from lchaimweekly.org/cgi-bin/calendar?holiday=tishrei7010201

6 In his exploration of the mountains in Matthew's gospel, Donaldson notes a link between the Mount of Olives and the mount of commissioning in Galilee, with the recurring phrase 'the end of the

age' (compare Matthew 24:3 and 28:20): Terence L. Donaldson, *Jesus on the Mountain: A study in Matthean theology* (JSOT Press, 1985).

7 For an archaeological perspective on the story, see Shimon Gibson, *The Final Days of Jesus: The archaeological evidence* (HarperOne, 2009). For a dramatic reimagining, see Richard Beard, *Lazarus is Dead* (Vintage Books, 2012).

8 For an overview of scholarship on John's gospel, see Gerard S. Sloyan, *What Are They Saying About John?* (Paulist Press, 2006). Parts of this chapter are indebted to Mayes, *Beyond the Edge*.

9 See Sandra M. Schneiders, 'The resurrection (of the body) in the fourth gospel' in John R. Donahue (ed.), *Life in Abundance: Studies of John's gospel in tribute to Raymond E. Brown* (Liturgical Press, 2005).

10 Indeed, the most typical form of Jewish prayer is the *berakhah*, the blessing of God for his gifts: 'Blessed are you, Lord God, King of the universe…'

11 David M. Carr, *The Erotic Word: Sexuality, spirituality and the Bible* (Oxford University Press, 2003), pp. 165–66.

12 This is explored in depth in Ann R. Windsor: *A King is Bound in the Tresses: Allusions to the Song of Songs in the fourth gospel* (Peter Lang, 1999).

13 See Barry A. Harvey, *Another City: An ecclesiological primer for a post-Christian world* (Trinity Press, 1999).

14 Philip Sheldrake, *Living Between Worlds: Place and journey in Celtic spirituality* (DLT, 1995), p. 30. See also Philip Sheldrake, *Spaces for the Sacred: Place, memory, and identity* (Johns Hopkins University Press, 2001).

15 'The Celtic psalter' in Robert Van de Weyer, *Celtic Fire: An anthology of Celtic Christian literature* (Darton, Longman & Todd, 1990).

Chapter 4 Encountering the fourth dimension: a sense of time

1 Margaret Davies, 'Structuring time in the fourth gospel' in her *Rhetoric and Reference in the Fourth Gospel* (JSOT Press, 1992), pp. 44–66.

2 Mark W.G. Stibbe, *John as Storyteller: Narrative criticism and the fourth gospel* (Cambridge University Press, 1994), p. 192.

3 In one place, John gives us foretaste, a proleptic anticipation of what is to come: John 11:2. Mary was the one who anointed the Lord with perfume and wiped his feet with her hair; her brother Lazarus was ill. Lazarus' illness and death do not happen until chapter 12. It alerts us to what is to come.

4 'Realised eschatology achieves in the gospel of John a greater dominance than any other New Testament document', from Oscar Cullmann, *Salvation in History*, tr. S.G. Sowers (Harper & Row, 1967), p. 269.

5 J. Philip Newell, *Listening for the Heartbeat of God: A Celtic spirituality* (SPCK, 1997), pp. 1, 7.

6 Esther de Waal, *The Celtic Way of Prayer: The recovery of the religious imagination* (Hodder and Stoughton, 2003), p. 55.

7 Extract is from Oliver Davies and Fiona Bowie (eds), *Celtic Christian Spirituality: An anthology of medieval and modern sources* (SPCK, 1997), p. 42. See also David Adam, *The Cry of the Deer: Meditations on the hymn of St Patrick* (Triangle, 1987).

8 Alexander Carmichael (ed.), *Carmina Gadelica III* (Scottish Academic Press, 1976), p. 53.

9 Kitty Muggeridge (tr.), *The Sacrament of the Present Moment: Jean-Pierre de Caussade* (Fount, 1996). He sought to counter the heresy of Quietism, which taught that the surest way to union with God was to foster a state of utter passivity before God, necessitating a complete withdrawal from the world, the annihilation of the human will and a cessation of all human effort, in the search to become totally available to God.

10 Muggeridge, *The Sacrament*, p. 46.

11 Muggeridge, *The Sacrament*, p. 75.

12 Muggeridge, *The Sacrament*, p. 40.

13 Muggeridge, *The Sacrament*, p. 54.

14 Muggeridge, *The Sacrament*, p. 109.

15 Eckhart Tolle, *The Power of Now: A guide to spiritual enlightenment* (New World Library, 2010), p. 61.

16 Thich Nhat Hanh, *The Miracle of Mindfulness* (Rider, 2015), p. 11.

Chapter 5 Feeling intensity, touching infinity

1 Gerard Manley Hopkins, 'The Blessed Virgin compared to the air we breathe', from hopkinspoetry.com.

2 General Synod of the Church of England, *Revised Catechism* (SPCK, 2006).

3 Liberation theology has opened our eyes to the ways in which God reveals his kingdom and his presence precisely through the poor: see, for example, Leonardo Boff, *Jesus Christ Liberator: Critical Christology for our times* (Orbis, 1978).

4 Thomas Merton, *Seeds of Contemplation* (Anthony Clarke, 1961), p. 2.

5 Stephen Voorwinde, *Jesus' Emotions in the Gospels* (T & T Clark, 2011), p. 151.

6 See, for example, Richard Buckner, *The Joy of Jesus: Humour in the gospels* (Canterbury Press, 1993); Michael Frost, *Jesus the Fool: The mission of the unconventional Christ* (Hendrickson, 2010); Jean Maalouf, *Jesus Laughed and Other Reflections on Being Human* (Sheed & Ward, 1996); Sherwood E. Wirt, *Jesus, Man of Joy* (Harvest House Publishers, 1999).

7 Culpepper, *Anatomy of the Fourth Gospel*, p. 112.

8 Voorwinde, *Jesus' Emotions*, p. 211.

9 There has been much debate over the centuries about 'divine impassibility' – the idea that God cannot suffer or experience emotions like pleasure or pain.

10 In the Synoptics, we recall Jesus weeping over Jerusalem (Luke 19:41). Hebrews 5:7 puts it: 'In the days of his flesh, Jesus offered up prayers and supplications, with loud cries and tears.'

11 Kallistos Ware, *The Orthodox Way* (St. Vladimir's Seminary Press, 1995), p. 10.

12 The three quotations above are from Kimberley Christine Patton and John Stratton Hawley (eds), *Holy Tears: Weeping in the religious imagination* (Princeton University Press, 2015).

13 References are paragraph numbers in Thomas Corbishley, *The Spiritual Exercises of St Ignatius Loyola* (Anthony Clarke, 1973). See also David L. Fleming, *The Spiritual Exercises of St Ignatius: A literal translation and a contemporary reading* (The Institute of Jesuit Sources, 1978).

14 See Herbert Alphonso, *Discovering Your Personal Vocation: The search for meaning through the spiritual exercises* (Paulist Press, 2001).

15 I am indebted to Maureen Conroy RSM for the contents of this paragraph. See her *Journey of Love: God moving in our hearts and lives* (Upper Room Spiritual Center, 1993).

16 I am grateful to Sue Cash for this approach to the *examen*.

17 ourcatholicprayers.com/suscipe.html

18 Our extract is from *Julian of Norwich: Showings* (trans. E. Colledge and J. Walsh; SPCK, 1978).

Chapter 6 Glimpsing glory

1 For an excellent reflection on intercession, see J. Neville Ward, *The Use of Praying* (Epworth Press, 1967).

2 'Hymn on Faith, 3' in Sebastian P. Brock, *The Luminous Eye: The*

spiritual world vision of St Ephrem the Syrian (Cistercian Publications, 1992), p. 73.

3 'Hymn on the Church, 29' in Brock, Luminous Eye, p. 75.

4 Richard of St Victor, De Sacramentis and The Mystical Ark (Paulist Press, 1979).

5 Rohr, The Naked Now, p. 28.

6 Meister Eckhart, 'Talks of instruction' in M.O'C. Walshe (tr.), Meister Eckhart: Sermons and treatises (Element Books, 1979), Vol. 3, p. 20.

7 Suzanne Noffke (tr.), The Prayers of St Catherine of Siena (Paulist Press, 1983), p. 180.

8 Quoted in William Johnston, The Inner Eye of Love: Mysticism and religion (Harper Collins, 1997), p. 24.

9 'Contemplative prayer is the simple expression of the mystery of prayer. It is a gaze of faith fixed on Jesus, an attentiveness to the Word of God, a silent love. It achieves real union with the prayer of Christ to the extent that it makes us share in his mystery' (Catechism of the Catholic Church, 2724).

10 See, for example, Lancelot Sheppard, Portrait of a Parish Priest: St John Vianney, the Curé d'Ars (Burns & Oates, 1960).

11 Pierre Teilhard de Chardin, Hymn of the Universe (Fount, 1969), pp. 27–28.

12 de Chardin, Hymn of the Universe, p. 29.

13 Pierre Teilhard de Chardin, Le Milieu Divin: An essay on the interior life (Fontana, 1957), pp. 145–46.

14 Ilia Delio, Christ in Evolution (Orbis, 2008), p. 180. See also M. Fox, The Coming of the Cosmic Christ (HarperOne, 1990).

15 Johann Baptist Metz, A Passion for God: The mystical-political dimension of Christianity (Paulist Press, 1998), p. 162.

16 Richard Rohr, Dancing Standing Still (Paulist Press, 2014).

Chapter 7 Hearing God's voice

1 For a recent reworking of the Triple Way in the psychology of spirituality, see Benedict J. Groeschel, Spiritual Passages: The psychology of spiritual development (Crossroad, 1995). See also Elizabeth Liebert, Changing Life Patterns: Adult development in spiritual direction (Chalice Press, 2000).

2 E. Allison Peers (tr.), St Teresa of Avila: Interior Castle (Sheed & Ward, 1974), pp. 6, 8. See a recent translation in Kieran Kavanaugh and Otilio Rodriguez (trs.), Teresa of Avila: The Interior Castle (Paulist Press, 1979).

3 Carolyn Humphreys, *From Ash to Fire: A contemporary journey through the Interior Castle of Teresa of Avila* (New City Press, 1992), p. 80.

4 Peers, *Teresa*, p. 33

5 Wearing my 'Spirituality Adviser' hat, I have been asking clergy what is helping their prayer.

6 Archbishops' Council, *mission-shaped church* (Church House Publishing, 2004), p. 104.

7 Richard Foster, *Celebration of Discipline* (Hodder and Stoughton, 1980), p. 28.

8 C.S. Lewis, *The Problem of Pain* (Fontana, 1976), pp. 81, 83.

9 Douglas V. Steere, *On Listening to Another* (Harper, 1955). See also Anne Long, *Listening* (Darton, Longman and Todd, 1990); Susan Hedahl, *Listening Ministry* (Fortress Press, 2001); Emma A. Justes, *Hearing Beyond Words: How to become a listening pastor* (Abingdon Press, 2010).

Chapter 8 Tasting eternity

1 It is not always possible to know whether these derive from Jesus himself or reflect the situation faced by the Christian communities for whom the gospels were first written.

2 Though the reference to the Spirit is not explicit here, the imagery of water and Spirit is a key theme in John's gospel (John 3; John 7).

3 Sang Hyun Lee, *From a Liminal Place: An Asian American theology* (Fortress Press, 2010), p. 47.

4 No doubt Matthew preserves an original aspect of the Lord's Prayer when he puts it: 'Forgive us our debts, as we also have forgiven our debtors' (Matthew 6:12).

5 George A. Maloney, *Intoxicated with God: The fifty spiritual homilies of Macarius* (Dimension Books, 1980).

6 Hilarion Alfeyev, *The Spiritual World of Isaac the Syrian* (Cistercian Publications, 2000), p. 249.

7 Sue Woodruff, *Meditations with Mechthild of Magdeburg* (Bear & Company, 1982), p. 88.

8 Caroline W. Bynum, *Jesus as Mother: Studies in the spirituality of the High Middle Ages* (University of California Press, 1982), p. 202.

9 Kieran Kavanaugh and Otilio Rodriguez, *The Collected Works of St John of the Cross* (Institute of Carmelite Studies, 1991), p. 475.

10 Quoted in John Meyendorff, *St Gregory Palamas and Orthodox Spirituality* (St Valdimir's Seminary Press, 1974), p. 49.

11 Teresa of Avila, *Interior Castle* (Sheed and Ward, 1974), IV, 2, 2. See

also E. Allison Peers in *Mother of Carmel: A portrait of St Teresa of Jesus* (Laing Press, 2003), p. 54. See also Teresa's *Life*, chapter XI.

12 Teresa of Avila, *Interior Castle,* p. 37. For a further exploration of the archetypal elements of water and wind, see Andrew D. Mayes, *Learning the Language of the Soul: A spiritual lexicon* (Liturgical Press, 2016).

13 Brother Roger, *Struggle and Contemplation* (SPCK, 1973), p. 31.

14 Pedro Casaldaliga and Jose Maria Vigil, *The Spirituality of Liberation* (Burns & Oates, 1994), p. 29.

15 St Chrysostom's 'Homilies on the gospel of St Matthew' in *Nicene and Post-Nicene Fathers: Part 10* (Kessinger Publishing, 2004).

16 St Augustine, 'Sermon 272' in Daniel Doyle (ed.) and Edmund Hill (tr.), *Essential Sermons: The works of Saint Augustine* (New City Press, 2007).

17 Brother Roger, *Festival* (SPCK, 1971), pp. 15–16, 131; adapted to use inclusive language.

Chapter 9 Welcoming the aroma of heaven

1 Dominika A. Kurek-Chomycz, 'The fragrance of her perfume' in *Novum Testamentum*, 52:4 (2010), pp. 334–54.

2 Raymond Brown, *The Gospel According to John*, vol. 2 (Geoffrey Chapman, 1966), p. 940.

3 James B. Nelson, *Body Theology* (Westminster/John Knox Press, 1992), p. 194–95.

4 Susan Harvey, *Scenting Salvation* (University of California Press, 2006). See also Vigen Guroian, *The Fragrance of God* (DLT, 2007).

5 Origen, *Commentary on Song of Songs.*

6 Sebastian Brock (tr.), *Saint Ephrem the Syrian: Hymns on paradise* (St Vladimir's Seminary Press, 1990), 11:13.

7 'May the fragrance of Jesus fill this place' by Graham Kendrick, copyright © 1986 Thankyou Music (Adm. by Capitol CMG Publishing worldwide excl. UK and Europe, adm. by Integrity Music, part of the David C. Cook family, songs @integritymusic.com).

Chapter 10 Reawakening: life in all its fullness

1 Archbishops' Council, *Services of Initiation* (Church House Publishing, 1998), pp. 164–65.

BRF

Transforming
lives and communities

Christian growth and understanding of the Bible

Resourcing individuals, groups and leaders in churches for their own spiritual journey and for their ministry

Church outreach in the local community

Offering two programmes that churches are embracing to great effect as they seek to engage with their local communities and transform lives

The Gift of Years

Teaching Christianity in primary schools

Working with children and teachers to explore Christianity creatively and confidently

Children's and family ministry

Working with churches and families to explore Christianity creatively and bring the Bible alive

parenting for faith

Visit **brf.org.uk** for more information on BRF's work

brf.org.uk

The Bible Reading Fellowship (BRF) is a Registered Charity (No. 233280)